# WELL

# DISCIPLINED

# TO

# EXCEL

By

Chrispin Ntungo

authorHOUSE™

*1663 Liberty Drive, Suite 200*
*Bloomington, Indiana 47403*
*(800) 839-8640*
*www.AuthorHouse.com*

First published by AuthorHouse 10/13/05

ISBN: 1-4208-7624-4 (sc)

Printed in the United States of America
Bloomington, Indiana

This book is printed on acid-free paper.

# Dedication

To Mutende, Chawezi, Mbawemi, Myazwe and my
own Mrs Universe, Grace. Your understanding is
much appreciated. And my love is guaranteed.

# Acknowledgements

I sincerely thank all Thursday with Chrispin Ntungo (TwCN) readers and particularly the following family, friends, and associates for sharing their expertise, ideas, materials, hugs and encouraging words.

My wife Grace Ntungo, Dr. K.C. Prince Asagwara, Vimbai Dune, Owen Chitohwa, Juanita Desouza-Huletey, Mwaka Kaonga, Gacheri Ann Dyck, Dr. Trust Beta, Jim Kasule, Isaac Katoyo, Delphin Mutaka, Dr. Edward Onyebuchi, Roger Amenyogbe, Hlezipi Sy, Robert Nguni, Willis Muhanga, Bose Agbayewa, my team and colleagues at TwCN, and Charter Kidzugane.

# Table of Contents

I Love Canada ........................................................................... 1

Our City, Our Share ............................................................... 4

African Community Women Lead the Way in Education .............. 7

Don't Be Deceived By Party Colors: Know The Principles ........... 10

Merry Christmas and a Happy New Year ....................................... 21

The Hugs and Hugs I Will Always Cherish .................................. 23

Someone in Zambia is Not Doing the Right Thing ....................... 28

When Leading Zambia Becomes Tough, Guard Against
Leadership Frustration .............................................................. 32

Two Hundred Fifty Million of Government Dollars Recklessly
Spent! Who Cares? ................................................................... 37

"Celebrating Growth and Learning" ........................................... 40

Building an African Community with a Prosperous Future ........ 43

Kofi Atta Annan - An African Son Deserving Ovation .................. 48

African Community Leaders Demonstrate Passion for Unity and
Prosperity ............................................................................... 52

Behind Federal Government's Budget Lines ................................ 56

Barriers to Success .................................................................. 61

Immigration: The Professional Group ....................................... 66

Me! A Leader? ......................................................................... 69

Well Disciplined To Excel .......................................................... 74

Destructive Challenges Confronting Our Youths ........................ 78

Empowering Kids To Be Responsible Youths - Part 1 ................. 83

Empowering Kids To Be Responsible Youths - Part 2 ................. 88

Just What Kind of Parent Are You? ........................................... 92

Election Time! One Opportunity for Networking ........................ 95

Husband! Bring Out The Personal Best Out Of Her ................... 98

On Jan Lamprecht ................................................................... 101

On Jan Lamprecht: Rejoinder ................................................... 105

Why Black People Struggle - A Perspective ................................... 108

Reflecting on the Manitoba Election and Marathon ..................... 117

Sudan: Too Much Talk, Little or Misplaced Action, No Improvement ........................................................................... 122

Time with Darci Lang.......................................................... 127

The World's Worst Evils ........................................................ 130

When Balance Is An Imperative.............................................. 134

Why So Many of Us Relate to Barack Obama............................. 138

Dual Citizenship: A Win-Win Strategy - Part 1 .......................... 144

Dual Citizenship: A Win-Win Strategy - Part 2........................... 148

No Scary Dreams for Ambitious Optimists ................................ 154

Olympic Games! Where The Truly Powerful Shine? ................... 158

We Can Do Better For Newcomers and the Community ............. 161

It's School Time! What Are You Planning To Study This School Year? ..................................................................................... 165

African-Canadian Community System for Support, Integration and Networking - Part 1................................................... 169

African-Canadian Community System for Support, Integration and Networking - Part 2................................................... 174

African-Canadian Community System for Support, Integration and Networking - Part 3................................................... 180

The Looming Identity Crisis.................................................. 191

The Secret of America's Mighty ............................................. 194

Your Money Adds Up to US$45 Billion a Year, Wow! ................. 197

Dreams................................................................................ 202

A Mandate To Complete The War, Hopefully! ........................... 205

Why You Should Hire Me, a Visible Minority............................ 208

ACCHC Project - Expectations and Reality ............................... 211

One Big Secret for Overseas African Business Success ............... 217

Celebrate the African Spirit .................................................. 222

Unity: the Master Key to Achieving the African Centre in Manitoba.............................................................................. 224

TwCN Celebrates One Year of Achievement – Part 1 ................. 227

TwCN Celebrates One Year of Achievement – Part 2 ................. 233

# I Love Canada

I cannot help it but to be thankful that my family and I have adopted Canada as our country. This is a country that has been voted by the United Nations on more than one occasion as the best country to live in. No wonder Paul Martin, the newly elected leader of the Liberal Party, and soon to be Canadian Prime Minister said he is proud. I believe he reflects the feeling of many other Canadians.

Just consider what Canada has to offer, in the spirit of Thursday with Chrispin Ntungo, focusing on Paul Martin's vision for Canada.

Canada offers, in Paul Martin's words, "endless glowing strings of cities, towns, and homesteads. When the stunning features of Canada stare at you, you see there exquisite variety, magnitude and ruggedness—and beauty. It is a palette of enormous colour and range. But more than that it is a profile of character, our character seen from above."

It is the character of Canada expressed by Paul Martin that makes me love it. Canada provides politicians that reason with the people. They recognize that the mission of government is to turn the national will, that is, the will of the people toward great accomplishment. Politicians listen to the people and set objectives and build consensus to achieve these objectives despite differences amongst them. Paul Martin promises to provide new politics of achievement.

Politics of achievement will involve building on Canadian treasured values and using ingenuity and innovation to expand the personal and national growth frontier. Politics of achievement, as summarized from Paul Martin's speech, will include:

1. Strengthening the social foundations of Canadian life—pension plan and universal health care systems. These foundations are the cornerstones of Canadian identity, pride and values.
2. Putting an end to regional discord and intergovernmental bickering, hence uniting the country's regions and their leaders.
3. Maintaining the sense of nationhood that is at ease with the Canadian identity of multicultural diversity and linguistic duality.
4. Increasing Canada's influence in the world working to ensure that the global institutions of the future are suffused with values Canadians treasure—rule of law, liberty, democracy, equality of opportunity and fairness.
5. Expressing the concerns of Canadians about the poor and underprivileged of the world; the frightened and helpless victims of battle-torn societies; the sick and vulnerable without healthcare and education.
6. Running a government that is accountable. A government that treats tax payers money like personal money, because it is.
7. Building an economy driven by individual ingenuity and creativity; which means having an education system that is second to none and committing to the pursuit of excellence and innovation.
8. Creating high quality jobs that will offer higher wages.
9. Increasing the strength of the new Canadian currency; that of ideas and discoveries.
10. Improving the quality of care for the less privileged among Canadians—children, the elderly. Hauling down the barriers which marginalize individuals with physical and mental disabilities.
11. Improving the quality of life for Canadians; letting Canadians feel quality by feeling good health, breathing clean air, tasting pure water from their taps.
12. Experiencing quality of life by seeing people working, with dignity, with good pay, with the opportunity to move ahead.

13.  Knowing quality of life by having Canadian families and children receive the schooling and higher education they need in today's world.
14.  It doesn't matter where you choose to live, for wherever you go you will find cities and regions thriving with energy.
15.  Having the ability to send messages to Ottawa through your Member of Parliament and not your member of Parliament bringing you messages from Ottawa.
16.  Having a leadership dedicated to building a society based on equality, not privilege; on duty, not entitlement. A society based on compassion and caring; not indifference or neglect.

Over the course of time, the African Community Secretariat plans to monitor how politics of achievement will be fulfilled.

Lastly, I liked how Paul Martin concluded his address. "It is in *Canadians* that the true meaning of Canada is found. Everything possible in the world is possible *in Canada*. Every dream that is dreamt can be fulfilled here." And the question is: Do you have a dream? If you do, then would you work to fulfill it? TwCN.

# Our City, Our Share

As immigrants to Canada, many of us are people whose presence is usually here in body. But in mind and spirit we are often present in our homelands. This affects our understanding and appreciation of where we live. Since where we live as immigrants is relatively better off, at least economically than where we came from, we become so comfortable and bother little about knowing the what, wheres, whys and hows of our relatively better city. In other words, we leave it to them to sort it out, trusting that all will work out better and whatever the outcome, they know better, and we know it will never be worse than what we left behind at home.

This reminds me of one of my Spanish-speaking friend, who once told me that when he landed in Canada, someone told him that Canada was not for him; rather it was for his children. He was told so, because his children would grow up in Canada, be well integrated and therefore, would be familiar with the issues and challenges. Consequently, they would, as Canadians, be in a position to positively contribute to the ideas and aspirations of Canadians. What about you and I? Would we really care about Winnipeg, our now home city?

Our home City of Winnipeg's preliminary Capital budget has just been tabled. I wonder how many of us are really concerned about what it contains. The Capital Budget is a six-year capital investment plan. Council adopts the first year of the plan for immediate implementation and the five-year forecast is adopted in principle.

Capital assets are generally defined as those with a cost exceeding $100,000 with minimum of 10-year life. There are some exceptions to this rule. For instance, major equipment or automated systems development projects are included in the capital budget, although there useful life may be less than 10 years. Land acquisition and local improvements are considered capital projects regardless of expected cost.

The Capital budget is used as a tool to authorize new projects. The City of Winnipeg's planned capital works for 2004, include:

- $50 million on upgrades to the sewage disposal system

- $38 million on the waterworks system, including an additional $26 million for the water treatment plant

- $38 million on street renewal

- $10.7 million for Community Services, of which $8 million is for the Millennium Library

The City also plans to be setting aside $5 million per year to pay for new strategic initiatives, such as the Kenaston Underpass and the Rapid Transit Corridor.

Whether or not these capital expenditures mean anything to anybody depends on what is present here between the mind and the body.

The City of Winnipeg's infrastructure includes sewer and water, roads, parks and facilities, land drainage, transit and any new investments. The Capital spending plan is modest compared to the city's overall infrastructure requirements. The City's annual infrastructure gap, the difference between what the City spends each year on capital projects and what is required to be spent, is estimated to be $188 million. Without being innovative this gap can easily be covered by simply raising property and business taxes. But being aware of the negative impact of high property and business taxes, the City, led by the Mayor Glen Murray, does not want to raise taxes. Instead, the City is trying to be very innovative and cover the gap, if possible even with lower taxes. And this is where Glen Murray's famous "new deal" comes in.

The City's current reliance on property and business based taxes is 42 percent and 6 percent, respectively. Through the "new deal" the City plans to reduce this reliance on property taxes to 23 percent and totally eliminate business taxes. As well, the city plans to increase consumption-based taxes from 3 percent to 28 percent and introduce environmental user fees to cover as much as 17 percent of budgetary requirements.

Overall, the "new deal" will bring in more revenue, which is badly needed to help revamp our city's infrastructure. There are many reasons why the new deal is appealing. One such reason is the fact that everyone who uses the city's infrastructure will contribute to its maintenance through user fees. This will include us the citizens of this city as well as our visitors. In a city nicknamed "Winterpeg," every nickel and dime counts. And if Glen Murray and his team would not know where to put it, which I doubt, we would recommend it goes to snow removal.

The "new deal" is not without its critics and hurdles. Mayor Glen Murray still has to negotiate with the Provincial and the Federal governments for a share of some taxes. The success of the "new deal" will largely depend on the outcome of these negotiations.

But if indeed the "new deal" would help to convert Winnipeg to fulfill Glen Murray's vision of a city that is beautiful and innovative, a city of choice, an economic hub, a city rich in arts and culture, a city with a vibrant downtown and interesting neighborhoods, a really clean and green city, I would have no problem saying go for it. Rather than moving and going to other cities to enjoy similar benefits I would rather see them accrue right here in my now adopted home city. It is our city and let's be happy to do our part and pay but our "fair" share. TwCN.

# African Community Women Lead the Way in Education

They are immigrants who come to Canada by way of marrying someone who is a student in Canada, or by way of being brought in as someone's niece, or by way of sponsorship by a brother or sister, or by way of being refugees. Some are married; others are single and single mothers. When they arrive they take a low profile, serving as babysitters, working in call centers, or hotels or with some cleaning company. In their humility they learn how the Canadian society works and its demands.

These women are but very patient with time. Those who are married are patient with their husbands. Those who come as babysitters are patient until such a time when they fulfill their duties to their unfailing Aunties. But there comes a time when these women, with some encouragement, resolve to go back to school. Of course having experienced a life of hard work, but with disproportionate reward, going back to school is the best option. To many it's a second chance. They heed the advice and adopt jeans and leather jackets, fold their sleeves, plait their hair and beat the path back to high school if they don't' already have a degree or to University if they already have a degree or high school certificate. They are unstoppable and determined and they know what they want.

I am talking about some African Community women in Winnipeg, Manitoba. I like what I observe, and I admire the outcome. With minimal encouragement, most have decided to go back to school. They are from everywhere in Africa—Sudan, Ghana, Zambia, DRC, Uganda, Ethiopia, Kenya, etcetera. They are all ceasing the opportunity presented them in the land of opportunity where dreams are fulfilled by all who are determined to fulfill them. They have seen the success and prosperity that comes with good education. They have seen the good jobs that those with Canadian education have. They have seen the opportunities presented particularly for women. Rather than sitting back and lamenting, and talking, they have banded in style and they are pursuing higher education in nursing, business, computers, etc. It is an encouraging picture indeed.

Every son and daughter, every husband, every brother, every sister, every aunt and uncle must be proud and rally behind these women and encourage them, support them, until they graduate. Children learn better from their mothers. As these women pursue higher education, they are serving as a good example to the African children. In the future the adage may as well be, "if mom did it, I will do it."

Winnipeg is a transformed city. After being here for over fifteen years, I have seen job prospects and opportunities for Africans become increasingly better. The only limiting factor is one's education. If you have the education you can be confident that you will get your dream job.

Moreover, it only takes one person to give an African Canadian a job. Someone who is familiar with Africans. This familiarity comes about as you go to school, and your classmates as well as your professors get to know how brilliant you are. It is these same people that in turn will provide you a job securing recommendation. As you spend time in school, build networks with your classmates. Take group projects as opportunities to build lasting friendships with your group mates. You will find the networks built at school last when you leave school.

Many Africans are still arriving in Winnipeg, and they will continue for many years to come. What advice will you give them? They may not believe it if you tell them your experience, especially if you say you actually once worked in the hotel or with a cleaning company. They come with high expectations, but they may be disappointed. Tell the whole story but conclude by saying it is the decision you made to go back to school and receive some education here that made the difference. Retraining is essential. And the good about it is that age is not a factor.

What about the money? Yes, you need money to go back to school. The fact is I have not seen one who has accumulated money first and then decided to go back to school. But most women I have seen have sacrificed the little they have towards education. Money is a funny possession. Whether you get educated or not you will always spend it. It is, therefore, necessary that if you have to spend it in your early years in Canada, you can as well spend it on education. That way, you increase your ability to earn a higher income when you become gainfully employed. Look at the money you spend to receive education as an investment. To find out more on how you can raise money for your education read Dr. Ntungo's "Turning Your Dreams into Reality: Personal Planning Guide for Success and Prosperity." You will find some really practical ideas to help you plan and save for your education.

As for new arrivals, the last word you might tell them is that they can do better. Ask them to have a dream to pursue, and then, cultivate patience as the virtue that will help them through the valleys and mountains they find and experience in Canada while working towards achieving their dream. Most Africans here have gone through this journey. It's no strange experience. To put a positive spin on it, even the first immigrants to Canada endured hardships. If you are not born here, life in the valley is the foundation and a necessary experience of being truly Canadian.

Lastly, to all the African Community women pursuing the higher education dream, thumbs up and hats off to you all. May success and prosperity find you in due time. TwCN.

# Don't Be Deceived By Party Colors: Know The Principles

It's still a major story, at least until the next federal election. The merger of the Progressive Conservatives and the Canadian Alliance. What is the big deal?

You have often heard of reporters speaking about political parties using such terms as the centre, the right and the left. Recently the merging of the Progressive Conservatives and the Canadian Alliance has been referred to as the right merging into one party. Why and what does it all mean for us? When it comes to an election each one of us is faced with a decision as to which candidate or party we should vote for or simply support.

First, in order to make an informed decision as to which party one should support let alone vote for, one must begin with having an understanding of the principles or philosophy of each party. Principles are core values that define the nature or the motivation of political parties. Labeling a party as either right, centre or left is determined by the principles to which the party subscribes. The focus of this week's TwCN is to shed some light on the principles that distinguish Canada's main political parties.

By LEFT is meant belief in socialist principles. Socialist principles promote communal production of wealth and total distribution of wealth to all individuals. Socialist principles are against individualism or concentration of wealth in the hands of the few individuals. Rather, individuals must be equally wealthy or poor, whichever way you choose to look at it. Socialists portray themselves as being cooperative, caring and compassionate. Socialist governments are characterized by creation of crown corporations and lower taxes for the middleclass. In Canada, the National Democratic Party or NDP is the left wing party. Table 1 shows the New Democratic Party Principles.

By RIGHT is meant belief in capitalist principles. Capitalist principles are for private ownership of property including means of production and distribution of wealth. The responsibility of government, in this case, is basically to create an enabling environment for businesses to operate efficiently and effectively. Conservative governments are characterized by privatization of crown corporations, lower taxes for businesses, but generally higher taxes for the working middleclass. In Canada, the PC and the Canadian Alliance are parties on the right. Now these two parties have merged into one party called the Conservative Party of Canada. Tables 2 and 3 show the Progressive Conservative and Canadian Alliance principles.

Both the left and the right have extremes. On the far left you find communist and Marxist-Leninist principles. I won't bother going into details, as it's common knowledge how ruinous these principles are. On the far right, you find the free-market people who believe in no government intervention, whatsoever, in running business. History shows that extremes on both the right and the left are disastrous for both individuals and states where they have been implemented.

Between the left and the right, of course, is the centre. And by CENTRE is meant liberal principles. Liberal principles borrow from both left and right. In other words, Liberals keep what works well or what is good for the people and/or the country, given the times, from both the right and the left. Liberals often demonstrate qualities of good leadership—working to ensure good performance of the economy and the well-being of individuals. Liberals would keep and manage what the left or right instituted if it works. They are good at changing what doesn't work, but are not so good at introducing totally new policies especially if the implication is radical change. In Canada, the Liberal Party is the centre party. Table 4 shows the Liberal Party Principles/Philosophy.

The current liberal leadership has commonly been referred to as "fiscally conservative" and "socially progressive." This means they are committed to running government on a balanced budget, and also maintaining the social institutions such as employment insurance, universal healthcare and the Canadian pension plan. On the contrary, if the liberals were described as capitalist progressive, they would be a type of government that would be working to undo the social institutions and putting them all in private hands.

As times change, individuals on the right and left may break. Liberals, however, are flexible, and therefore, have the ability to adapt and survive changing times.

What about elections? Elections always present an opportunity for parties to revisit their principles and communicate them to people through policies. During elections parties present platforms or policies indicating how they plan to deal with prevailing problems and issues of the day. And issues of the day differ from election to election. Voters change candidates and parties they support based on the platforms presented. However, one must bear in mind that platforms presented for elections purposes don't go contrary to the principles of the party. This is evidenced by promises made, but not fulfilled. Sometimes, promises made are contrary to the party's principles. When in power, the leadership decides to curve in and live by party principles leaving voters wondering what happened.

The PC and the CA have merged because they ascribe to similar principles. Unless you are a "die hard" for a particular party, you don't need to break. Rather you have the opportunity to aquaint yourself with the principles of all the major Canadian political parties, as well as problems and issues of the day. When you have the opportunity to vote, don't be deceived by party colors: know the principles and make an informed decision and vote wisely. TwCN.

## Table 1 - New Democratic Party Principles

**PREAMBLE**

The New Democratic Party believes that the social, economic and political progress of Canada can be assured only by the application of democratic socialist principles to government and the administration of public affairs.

The principles of democratic socialism can be defined briefly as:

1. That the production and distribution of goods and services shall be directed to meeting the social and individual needs of people within a sustainable environment and economy and not to the making of profit;

2. To modify and control the operations of the monopolistic productive and distributive organizations through economic and social planning. Towards these ends and where necessary the extension of the principle of social ownership;

3. The New Democratic Party holds firm to the belief that the dignity and freedom of the individual is a basic right that must be maintained and extended; and

4. The New Democratic Party is proud to be associated with the democratic socialist parties of the world and to share the struggle for peace, international co-operation and the abolition of poverty.

*Source: Constitution of the New Democratic Party of Canada, 2003*

## Table 2- Progressive Conservative Statement of Principles

The principles of the Progressive Conservative Party of Canada are:

1.  A belief in loyalty to a sovereign and united Canada governed in accordance with the Constitution of Canada, the supremacy of democratic parliamentary institutions and the rule of law;

2.  A belief in the equality of all Canadians;

3.  A belief in the freedoms of the individual, including freedom of speech, worship and assembly;

4.  A belief in our constitutional monarchy, the institutions of Parliament and the democratic process;

5.  A belief in the federal system of government as the best expression of the diversity of our country, and in the desirability of strong provincial and territorial governments;

6.  A belief that the best guarantors of the prosperity and well-being of the people of Canada are:
    a.  the freedom of individual Canadians to pursue their enlightened and legitimate self-interest within a competitive economy;
    b.  the freedom of individual Canadians to enjoy the fruits of their labour to the greatest possible extent; and
    c.  the right to own property.

7.  A belief that a responsible government must be fiscally prudent and should be limited to those responsibilities which cannot be discharged reasonably by the individual or others;

8.  A belief that it is the responsibility of individuals to provide for themselves, their families and their dependents, while recognizing that government must respond to those who require assistance and compassion;

9. A belief that the purpose of Canada as a nation state and its government, guided by reflective and prudent leadership, is to create a climate wherein individual initiative is rewarded, excellence is pursued, security and privacy of the individual is provided and prosperity is from a free competitive market economy;

10. A belief that the quality of the environment is a vital part of our heritage to be protected by each generation for the next;

11. A belief that Canada should accept its obligations among the nations of the world; and

12. A belief that good and responsible government is attentive to the people it represents and has representatives who at all times conduct themselves in an ethical manner and display integrity, honesty and concern for the best interest of all.

13. The leadership of the Party is accountable to its Members for ensuring that policies espoused by the Party are guided by these principles.

*Source: Constitution of the Progressive Conservative Party of Canada 2002*

## Table 3- Canadian Alliance Statement Of Principles

1. We believe in a sovereign and united Canada as a balanced federation of equal provinces and citizens, loyal to our Constitutional monarchy, governed by the democratic institutions of Parliament, and subject to the rule of law.

2. We believe in the inherent value and dignity of the individual citizen, that all citizens are equal before the law and entitled to fundamental justice, and that those citizens have certain fundamental and immutable freedoms, namely: freedom of speech and the freedom to advocate, without fear of intimidation or suppression, public policies which reflect their most deeply held values; freedom of religious belief and practice; freedom of peaceful assembly and the freedom of choice of association; and the freedom to own, enjoy, and exchange private property in a free market.

3. We believe that the family is the essential building block of a healthy society, and the primary mechanism by which Canadians pass on their values and beliefs to the next generation; and that because of this unique importance, the family must be strengthened and protected from unnecessary intrusions by government.

4. We believe that Canadians have a personal and social responsibility to care and provide for the basic needs of those who are genuinely unable to care and provide for themselves; and that this responsibility begins with the family and extends from there to voluntary private organizations.

5. We believe in limited government that undertakes only prudent and constructive change; that the proper role of government is to create an environment of political and economic freedom within which the citizens can pursue their own legitimate self-interest; and that government should do only those things which citizens, individually or collectively, cannot do for themselves.

6. We believe that the necessary functions of government should be delegated to the appropriate order of government closest to the people, that the division of powers among different orders of government must be respected, and that all citizens are entitled to benefit equally, without prejudice, from the services offered by government.

7. We believe that political parties should be guided by stated values and principles which are shared by their Members; that the people's elected representatives exist to serve their electors honestly, ethically, and with concern for all; that their duty to their electors supersedes their obligations to their political parties or personal_views; that they should treat public moneys as funds held "in trust" to be spent wisely and with prudence; and that law-makers and the institutions of government must be subject to the same laws as apply to the people themselves.

8. We believe that government should reflect the will of the citizens, and that this will should be expressed through democratic processes including: free and fair elections in which the citizens choose their own representatives to govern them through representative and accountable institutions; the power of the citizens to recall elected representatives who violate their mandates; the power of the citizens directly to initiate the legislative process; and the power of the citizens directly to decide on matters of public policy by referendum.

9. We believe that effective representative government is best provided by a balanced bicameral legislature consisting of: the House of Commons, with Members evenly distributed on the basis of the population distribution in the country, elected by the people of their constituencies; and the Senate, elected to represent the interests of the Provinces and Territories as a complement and counter-balance to the population distribution of the Commons; with equal representation determined through Constitutional discussions with the Province and the Territories, with both of these bodies held accountable to their electors.

10. We believe that government must act for the benefit of future generations as much as for the present, maintaining policies that will nurture and develop the people's knowledge and skills, preserve a stable, healthy and productive society, and ensure the responsible development and conservation of our environment and natural heritage.

*Source: Constitution of the Canadian Reform Conservative Alliance 2000*

## Table 4 - Liberal Party Philosophy

1. The Liberal Party of Canada is committed to the view that the dignity of each individual man and woman is the cardinal principle of democratic society and the primary purpose of all political organization and activity in such a society.

2. It is dedicated to the principles that have historically sustained the Party: individual freedom, responsibility and human dignity in the framework of a just society, and political freedom in the framework of meaningful participation by all persons. The Liberal Party of Canada is bound by the Constitution and the Charter of Rights and Freedoms and is committed to the pursuit of equality of opportunity for all persons, to the enhancement of our unique and diverse cultural community, to the recognition that English and French are the official languages of Canada, and to the preservation of the Canadian identity in a global society.

3. In accordance with this philosophy, the Liberal Party of Canada subscribes to the fundamental rights and freedoms of persons under the rule of law and commits itself to the protection of these essential values and their constant adaptation to the changing needs of modern Canadian society.

4. The Liberal Party of Canada recognizes that human dignity in a democratic system requires that all citizens have access to full information concerning the policies and leadership of the Party, the opportunity to participate in open and public assessment of such means, such modifications of policies and leadership as they deem desirable to promote the political, economic, social, cultural and general well-being of Canadians.

5. To realize this objective, the Liberal Party of Canada strives to provide a flexible and democratic structure whereby all Canadians can obtain such information, participate in such assessment and militate for such reform through open communications, free dialogue and participatory action both electoral and non-electoral.

*Source: Liberal Party Constitution and Documents.*

*Thoughts Of Some Great Liberal Leaders*

*"I am a Liberal. I am one of these who think that everywhere, in human things, there are abuses to be reformed, new horizons to be opened up, and new forces to be developed." - Sir Wilfrid Laurier, June 1877*

*"Liberal philosophy places the highest value on freedom of the individual. The first consequence of freedom is change. A Liberal can seldom be a partisan of the status quo. He tends to be a reformer – attempting to move society, to modify its institutions, to*

*liberate its citizens. The liberal is an optimist at heart who trusts people. He does not see man as an essentially perverse creature, incapable of moral progress and happiness. Nor does he see him as totally or automatically good. He prizes man's inclination to good but knows it must be cultivated and supported. While understanding as well as any other man the limits of government and the law, the liberal knows that both are powerful forces for good, and does not hesitate to use them." - The Right Honourable Pierre Elliott Trudeau, April,1974*

*"Liberalism is now, and has been since its beginnings, the one political philosophy that has promoted political freedom, cultural pluralism and economic democracy. Liberals believe, first of all, that the rights of the individual are paramount to those of the state - any state. We believe all individuals must be accorded the opportunity to fashion their own lives and grow to the limit of their own potential. We believe in promoting an equality of the human condition. Equality in employment, education, training, regardless of colour, creed, sex or family background. We believe that responsibilities go with those rights. We have a duty to exercise our rights in order to preserve the rights of others. We have a responsibility to serve the commonwealth, and to contribute to the governance of a free community, and to ensure with a vigilance that it remain free." - The Right Honourable John N. Turner, September, 1987*

*"The history of the Liberal Party is the history of a political party which has acted as an agent of change in Canada. From Laurier, who opened the West with a farsighted immigration policy; King, who began to build a national system of social security; St. Laurent, who completed Confederation with the entry of Newfoundland and who built a strong prosperous economy based on a mix of the public and private sector; Pearson, who added to the social security system with Medicare; Trudeau, who enshrined bilingualism and*

*the place of French Canada and who fought for and won a Charter of Rights and Freedoms - the Liberal Party has always been at the forefront of social change in Canada" - The Honourable Jean Chrétien, November 1991*

*"The Liberal Party offers a vision of Canadian success in the 21st century that reflects shared Canadian values. Values of fairness, tolerance and sharing. Ours is a vision in which all Canadians have an equal chance to realize their dreams and fulfill their unique potential. We believe Canada must have a strong national government that makes decisions based on the needs and aspirations of all Canadians. We have the plan that will make our vision a reality. That will keep Canada the best country in the world-now and in the future."*

*- The Right Honourable Jean Chrétien, November 2000*

# Merry Christmas and a Happy New Year

I have heard the words "Merry Christmas" and a "Happy New Year" and various versions of them all my life, and I truly believe you have heard them too all your life. This year like every year, as greetings and best wishes continue to arrive at my desk, I cannot help but to spend some moments pondering what they all mean. In so doing, I provide myself opportunity to appreciate the reason for Christmas and also the reason for the New Year.

What comes first, merry Christmas or the New Year? If you look on your calendar you will notice that the New Year comes first. This is important to know. Ideally to have a merry Christmas, you must have had a happy "new" year. By Christmas, the year is actually old and coming to an end. If you have extra money left towards the end of the year you spend all that on gifts for your beloved ones and friends. The celebration of Christmas, in as much as its reason is for Christ having been born into this world, is an opportunity to remember God's grace for you and your family which kept you health and strong throughout the year. You conclude the year by being merry or happy or joyous as the year ends.

Last weekend, I had the opportunity to attend a Christmas social of some kind. The organizer of the social provided some youth opportunity to speak up. One female youth, whose mom recently moved to Canada, said something that got many a people in the room thinking. She said, "You can take me out of Zimbabwe, but you can't take Zimbabwe away from me." I think that this is true for most immigrants.

21

At Christmas, when I look at how much gifts are exchanged, I can't help but to think of the children in parts of the world without commercialized Christmas. How much they need, and how much they would appreciate receiving a gift. Recently, I watched one of the most powerful and influential women in the world sharing a story on Larry King Live of how she visited Africa. She had planned to give gifts to one million African children. But when she went to Africa, because of lack of logistical support, she only managed to give gifts to fifty thousand children. The woman said that what made her happy was the opportunity to see the joy on African kids and how genuinely appreciative they were. Apparently these kids called her Mother Oprah.

The New Year provides people opportunity to plan for life again. You have heard of the famous phrase "new year resolutions." This phrase is actually very reasonable and helpful, but only for those individuals who take their life seriously. It is a challenge for most people to sit and resolve to achieve something in a given year. Some people fear to be disappointed if they fail to stick to their resolutions. Others opt to say don't take life seriously. Yet a few believe they must have resolutions and plan their year. I hope you are one of the few.

This year alone I have had five friends of mine turn forty. The big Four-O is a special birthday for most people. Of the five friends of mine, only one planned a special trip to the Caribbean to enjoy a cruise. When I heard about it, I had to find a picture of a Cruise Ship. They are magnificent. Most people may think they are made for movie actors and a few millionaires here and there. Far from it. Everyone can go for a cruise. It starts with a new year's resolution.

For my friend, her cruise trip did not come as a gift or by chance. She planned and saved for this special milestone in her life. But the cruise is just one example of the many things you can resolve to do and plan for. Think about your spiritual development, your family, your profession, your finances, your investments, your health, your education, etc. As many friends and family wish you a happy and prosperous New Year, don't let them down. Do something to show that their wishes are not falling on "hard" ears. But rather are being received by one who cares and is dedicated to turning dreams into reality. Please enjoy the holiday season! TwCN

# The Hugs and Hugs I Will Always Cherish

I am back. But this place is too cold. For a month I constantly enjoyed 27 above zero, then suddenly I plunge myself into the 40 below zero weather. This is crazy!

My vacation was exceptional. It came after a little more than ten years of being away from home—Zambia. When I started off, I was well lost. I didn't know what to expect. But reality hit me when I safely arrived in Lusaka, Zambia. Coming off the plane I was welcome by warm sunny weather, temperature around 27 above zero and best of all green vegetation. While in the air I could hardly see any buildings, only some elaborate patterns of Lusaka farms. Much of the city of Lusaka is buried in trees, which provide shade for people who mostly walk—its beautiful, but it also reminded me of why some people here think Africans live in the jungle. But it's not a jungle. Rather it's a typical African healthy green environment and it's beautiful.

Leaving the arrival lounge around 7:00 a.m., I found a mob of relatives waiting for me. It was hugs and kisses. I could recognize three or four of these people. But could not recognize the rest. These were my young brothers and sisters, nieces and nephews who had grown so much over the past ten years. As well some were my in-laws who are now part of my family because my brothers and sisters have married. It would take me the whole day to learn about them all and remember them all. At this point I had no plans of my own. I had left it to my brother to take care of my arrival plans. And the plan was such that I could touch four places on my way to my final destination where I would spend my first night.

So I started with my cousins' places in Chelston, Avondale and Jesmondine. On my way to Emmasdale and in the company of my cousins one from South Africa, we stopped for lunch at Manda Hill, Lusaka's most popular and famous shopping complex. It's beautiful. There I asked to have Fanta, my childhood drink, which unfortunately I cannot find here in Winnipeg. The lunch was superb and the Fanta still tasted good.

I reached my destination around 5:00 p.m. and the partying started almost immediately. It was an evening of charting, dancing, feasting and catching up. I had the opportunity to hear the rich Zambian music. It is good. But people danced to all kinds of music including notable artists from Democratic Republic of the Congo (DRC), Zimbabwe, and South Africa. Once in a while, I could think of how it would be when I meet mom and dad up in Mbala, Northern Province. My thoughts could reach so far, and somehow I could blame myself and ask, "Why did I take so long to see people who love me so much?" I experienced several emotional moments. But I am so grateful God granted me the opportunity to meet my beloved ones. And this was just the beginning of many enjoyable and memorable moments I would have with my family. It wasn't until past midnight that I decided I needed some rest.

I have a cousin who lives in South Africa who I had not met for 15 years. I did tell him that I would be visiting home for a month. So he decided to arrange his vacation so we could meet. He was a blessing to me. He came driving all the way from South Africa. And he drove a BMW. I have never had the opportunity to ride a BMW in Winnipeg. It took me a visit home to have the opportunity to ride in a BMW. Thanks Henry!

After two days in Lusaka, my cousin and I drove about 12 hours to reach my hometown—Mbala in Northern Province, and where my parents live. We arranged our travel such that we arrived in the morning around 10:00 a.m. Of all the people, I wanted to see most my Mom and Dad. But like in Lusaka, when I reached home, there were all these people, most of whom I couldn't recognize. Of course I saw my dad and we hugged and warmly greeted each other. My mom was nowhere to be seen. Being such a hard working mother she was away in the field. So dad had to send for her.

I was a little bit unsettled having not seen my mom. Then mom finally came. We hugged and hugged. I was so happy. She looked to be in better shape than I had actually expected. I could see my parents' faces glow with joy and some sense of unbelief. Finally they were there with their son they had not seen for a little over ten years. Which parent could not rejoice? Word of my arrival spread like fire. And people kept flocking down to greet me. For a moment I felt really special. The moment I longed for was finally here—a moment to be with my parents. I could not help but be grateful to God for his mercies and the opportunity to meet and see my parents again.

I spent one week with my parents. I showed them pictures of my family in Canada. My dad and I reviewed the family tree. I had the opportunity to ask dad some family questions and dad answered and explained to me everything I needed to know.

Following my busy itinerary, my next stop was my wife's hometown—Chipata, Eastern Province. In order to go to Eastern Province I had to return to Lusaka, and then from Lusaka travel to Chipata. In Lusaka I met my wife's three brothers and a sister. I have never seen people who look so alike as my wife's siblings. I felt so at home for it seemed Grace had come along. I cherished the opportunity to sit down and chart with Grace's siblings. They look so alike and they constantly reminded me of my sweetheart. I had such a good feeling.

It's six hours drive to Chipata. Because I was going to my in-laws place I needed some warm company. So I had two brothers-in-law (Christopher and Mabvuto) accompany me. When Grace and I married, I was already in Canada. I didn't have the opportunity to meet any of her siblings to the extent that we would know each other. So visiting my wife's place, involved me meeting her siblings and other relatives for the first time and getting to know them really quick. My six hours travel afforded me the opportunity to know my two brothers-in-law. And they were good. They really cared for me and ensured my travel was enjoyable.

We reached Chipata around 2:00 a.m. We stayed at my sister-in-law's place for the night. I first met my sister-in-law (Martha) at my wedding back in 1993. However, I met my brother in marriage for the first time. We hugged and hugged. I enjoyed my brother's company because we come from the same home town. So we spoke our language. And sitting down and charting with my sister-in-law was yet another reminder that I was Grace's husband. I couldn't help, but cherish the moment. She also looked so much like my wife.

Every time was special, but the really special time I was looking forward to was the moment I would meet my father-in-law. It was another hour's drive to reach my father-in-law's place. This was a man, who just over one year ago had lost his beloved wife—my mother-in-law—in a traffic accident. So I really wanted to see him and know how he was coping.

When we arrived home, we didn't find him. He had gone visiting in the neighborhood. In the meantime, my in-laws suggested taking me around the farm. I enjoyed the tour seeing maize, groundnuts and tobacco fields. We took some pictures. While on tour, my father-in-law returned from his visit and met us by the fields. He was not expecting to see us then. Suddenly, he recognized his sons, and it immediately dawned on him that his son-in-law had arrived. The man burst with joy. We greeted each other joyously. I was so happy to see him, and especially to see he was so joyous and I could see his face glow with joy. It had been ten years. But now here he was with his son-in-law. It was beautiful. The son, my brother-in-law, decided that we continue with our tour, and advised him to proceed home and that we would join him later.

We toured the farm from deep down on the Zambian side all the way to the border with Malawi. I could not believe when my in-laws told me that we were standing on the border. Of course there was nothing really special, rather than just a gravel road along the border. I looked both sides of the border—into Malawi and into Zambia. I thought it was really interesting.

At sunset we returned home. I was very impressed when I saw that the farmhouse had a mounted solar panel that was used for lighting. My father-in-law and I spent some time together sharing something about Canada with him and learning much about his life in retirement. In the mean time, two sisters-in-law (Joyce and Rebecca) were occupied ensuring that we had supper and warm water for evening baths. We eventually retired to bed around 10:00 p.m.

Following morning, as expected was sunny and really warm. The first order of business was to pay my respects to my late mother-in-law. So, according to tradition, I had some elders from the neighborhood take me to the cemetery. They explained to me the circumstances surrounding my mother-in-law's death. It was an emotional moment. As children, we will always live to remember her. She lives in each of her children for they all take their facial appearance as well as compassionate values after her.

My in-laws were all just amazing. The beautiful smiles, soft speaking, warm hugs, and the demonstrated care all testify to the fact that mother-in-law did instill in her children values money cannot buy. I salute them all. I can't help but be grateful that I happen to be part of this family. I am also happy that I did sit down with father-in-law and asked about all his children. As a result, I now know them all very well.

Pen and paper are not enough to express all my vacation experiences. But I will always cherish the time I spent with my parents, my father-in-law and all my beloved ones. Of course, my challenge is to visit home with my family. And I hope that this is a dream that will be fulfilled soon. I also learned it's never too expensive to visit home especially if your parents are still alive. I would do it at every opportunity. TwCN.

# Someone in Zambia is Not Doing the Right Thing

When you are considering Zambia, the evidence for economic development is not in what the government has funded, but in what the individual citizens have. And because what the government has funded is lacking, it appears someone is not doing the right thing for the people let alone the nation.

While vacationing in Zambia, I took time to observe evidence for economic development. I observed that while in Capital City Lusaka, you can get almost anything you need to have a decent living. You can find all kinds of food, all kinds of groceries, or kinds of household goods including living and bedroom accessories. You can live in a house with a sweeming pool. You can also get yourself any type of Germany or Japanese car. Most of the goods in Zambia are supplied from South Africa. Hats off to South Africa.

In today's world the ability to communicate fast is important. Much of communication in Zambia is by cell phone. I saw more variety of cell phones than I have seen in Winnipeg and the competitiveness of the industry is comparable to none in Winnipeg, Manitoba. Although so competitive, I found the cost of communication to still be very expensive especially across lines. The minimum can be as much as 50 US cents per minute.

Customers buy calling card units in US dollars in denominations of US$5 and US$10. But for every calling card unit you use, you get double the time of receiving calls and this time is cumulative. Most people use their phones for receiving calls. You can therefore, borrow someone's cell phone and use it to make your calls. The owner of the phone benefits by having a credit of more time to receive calls.

All the major roads out of Lusaka are well paved. These roads were paved using a grant from the Japanese government. And if you simply arrive and drive to State House or Canadian Embassy you might think you are in a well developed country. And you may be right from one perspective. You have to visit places where the common man lives to see the whole picture. The sad story begins about a stone throw away from the major roads as you head into compound residential areas. Two things made me really sad. The pot holed roads and the refuse on the sides of the roads.

I also visited a couple of markets. I was very impressed when I observed that I could find anything I could think of—food, hardware, gifts, etc. But the structures and the environment in which these commodities were being traded disappointed me. From what I saw, I could conclude that individual Zambians are working so hard ensuring that transportation; merchandize and personal services are available for all who could afford. I could, however, deduce that someone somewhere in a government office was not doing their job to ensure that the city has the infrastructure it needs for its citizens to use, as well as to ensure that the environment is clean to guarantee public health.

Fortunately, I knew someone at Zambia Revenue Authority (ZRA). ZRA is an organization similar to Customs and Revenue Canada. This organization is being showcased in all of Africa as a model for an effective and efficient revenue collection authority. I had a discussion with one Commissioner at the authority. I particularly wanted to find out if the money the authority collects is not sufficient enough to meet government needs for expenditures. The official told me that the authority has always collected money to meet all the expenditure targets of the government. It was pleasing to hear such reassuring words.

As an ordinary citizen, I would like to believe that government expenditures must include expenditures on infrastructure including roads, hospitals, schools, parks, policing equipment, etc. And this is what disappointed me most. Everywhere I traveled in Zambia—Kabwe, Ndola, Kasama, Mbala, Petauke and Chipata—I especially observed the quality of the infrastructure everyone expects the government to fund and maintain. I am sorry to say I didn't see much evidence that the government is spending any money to maintain this infrastructure. This makes me sad. If I were to blame someone it would be someone in a government office. And I would say the government is not doing the right thing. They have their priorities misplaced.

In Zambia elected Mayors and Council govern cities. Among other responsibilities, the council is responsible for maintaining streets as well as the city environment. Therefore, when streets are not maintained and there is refuse in public places, one cannot go wrong pointing a finger at the local government. Also, Zambia has a central government. The representative of the central government at each town is an appointed government official called the District Administrator or Commissioner. If these central government officials were responsible they would advocate and ensure that schools, hospitals, major roads and the environment in their towns are maintained and kept in magnificent condition. But evidence of effective and responsible governance is hard to see.

What would one make of all this? Not withstanding the structure of the Zambian government, it appears to me that Zambia has a government that is more consumption oriented than investment oriented. In other words, Zambia appears to have a government that spends most of its financial resources on salaries and fringe benefits of its staff, which include Members of Parliament (MPs) and civil servants. Some of the fringe benefits are pretty expensive. For instance, every MP receives an SUV or Pajero upon being elected. Hosts of civil servants attend seminars and conferences, travel first class and are paid abnormal allowances. Most of the money that is supposed to be earmarked for capital improvements ends up in individual's pockets dressed up as fringe benefits and allowances.

I had the opportunity to listen to the Zambian President Levy Mwanawasa open the August house of Parliament. After reading a line on infrastructure development, the President emphasized that he did not want to hear that the money has been used for seminars and conferences. In other words, the president wants to see tangible results. I take that to mean he wants to see improvements in the capital infrastructure of the country. And the president means good.

Unfortunately, the President cannot run each and every ministry so he has control over how resources are allocated and used. He must trust the people around him. For the President's dream to be achieved, one must hope that the people around the president are not spoilers.

Overall, Zambia will need a change of culture and attitude in order for it to move beyond consumption and into infrastructure investment. With a good plan and a responsible government, it will not be long to see the economic vibrancy of the people reflected in the strength and beauty of the infrastructure and the cleanliness of the environment. TwCN.

# When Leading Zambia Becomes Tough, Guard Against Leadership Frustration

G overning a developing country is not easy. It is actually so hard that if a governor lacks wisdom, it is very easy to get off course and make unreasonable utterances as an expression of frustration. This was the case with the Zambian president, who at the opening of a leadership development workshop for his cabinet and senior civil servants expressed his frustration by labeling the thousands of Zambians in the Diaspora as failures, incompetent and inefficient.

His utterance has undoubtedly left many a Zambian people home and abroad angry. Perhaps angry not because they think the president really means what he said, but rather that what he said is an expression of how little he knows about the impact of Zambians abroad both on the home economy as well as globally. And I need not go into directly responding to his remarks. Rather I would like to take the opportunity to point out some fundamental reasons why thousands of Zambians choose to live abroad rather than at home.

*A prophet is not welcome in his own town.*

The Zambian political economy is such that it favors and honors those in politics than professionals in education, health, business and science. Fortunately, politicians' capabilities and usefulness are limited to the local Zambian market. Professionals, on the other hand, are marketable on the international labor market. Rather than fight the injustices at home to the peril of their lives and families, most Zambian professionals choose to respond to labor market demands and go where they can contribute effectively and be most appreciated.

*Respect for human rights*

The Zambian president asked what the Zambians abroad are afraid of at home. There may not be imminent danger. But, unless you live in the guarded state house, the Zambian political and economic environment is not totally safe.

Zambians in power still have to go a long way to demonstrate that they can accommodate dissenting voices. Too many times we have seen those with dissenting voices lose their jobs or demoted from their political ranks. We have seen university students battered. We have seen independent minds reprimanded. To many educated Zambians, this is hard to take.

As well, Zambians must be free to travel and live anywhere they wish in the world. It is part of freedom of movement. But the president is alienating those in the Diaspora and threatening he cannot listen to them at a time they are not even challengers to his presidency. What would the case be if they were actually challengers?

*Employment, education and personal development opportunities*

The labour market in Zambia is such that it fails to gainfully reward professionals so that they can live on their incomes. So most professionals go outside Zambia to make a decent living.

As well the educational system in Zambia is such that it brings out so many grade 9s and grade 12s who with their levels of education cannot find any gainful employment in Zambia. Worse still there are no opportunities to upgrade their education. The same graduates when they leave Zambia are able to find opportunities to upgrade their studies, even up to university level, and are able to find gainful employment and lead meaningful lives. Who wouldn't take on such an opportunity? May be the Zambian statehouse wouldn't. If these people would be labeled failures at home, the president must be appreciative that at least they found a way to develop themselves and become productive citizens of the world.

And those who choose not to leave Zambia, where do they end up? Take up crime as their career? Become MMD party cadres without credentials or mishanga boys and terrorize the innocent? Is that the outcome the Zambian government wants of Zambian education? I am afraid not the Zambians abroad.

*Healthcare environment*

"What are they afraid of?" asked the president. The incumbent Zambian president was once involved in a car accident. Luckily he was vice-president at the time. He sought medical attention in South Africa. So it appears he wants all the other Zambians to be courageous and seek medical attention in Zambia while he himself and perhaps his family seek medical attention abroad. It is not fair.

The health environment at home is pathetic. And if Zambians in their right minds cannot be afraid, they may be labeled temporarily insane. And unfortunately Zambia has been hit hard by HIV/AIDS epidemic. There are still cholera cases in the capital city Lusaka where the president resides. This is sad. I feel for fellow Zambians who have to suffer these diseases.

The president must demonstrate leadership in mobilizing Zambians both at home and abroad to fight these health problems. Uttering such words as "personally I don't pay attention to such people" (Zambians abroad) is no good demonstration of credible leadership and concern for the country and its people. Remember most African countries achieved political independence by fighting from outside. Likewise, Zambia can and will achieve economic prosperity in the same way through capital transfers and investments from its nationals abroad. The president's challenge is to put in place a system that will track such capital flows and investments.

*Reasonable and effective leadership*

Zambians abroad have experienced reasonable and effective leadership. And they wish Zambian leaders could be the same.

Unfortunately, these leaders are not willing to learn. And where there is no learning, I am afraid there is no change and hence no development.

Zambians abroad are intelligent enough to notice that the problem at home is not that the country does not have money. Rather the big problem is the attitude of leaders and perhaps some of the people. The attitude that when you leave Zambia you have forsaken your people; the attitude that when you differ with the president you are an enemy; the attitude that when you make suggestions you are opposing the leadership. Unless such attitudes change, the impact of the efforts of all Zambians to develop Zambia will not be seen.

Why is it that it is so difficult to find trustworthy people to work with at home? Maybe the workshop should focus on teaching leaders values of honesty, integrity and truthfulness in their business dealings. Per adventure the people will learn from their leaders values of trust, integrity and honesty. So when help comes from sisters and brothers abroad, they can honestly account for it.

Living abroad is an eye opener for most Zambians. It is also a source of experience. When Zambians abroad speak, they are speaking with experience and a conviction that, with the right attitude, what they suggest can work because they have seen it work somewhere else. Zambians abroad are looking for reasonable and effective leaders at home, whom they can work with and together support the country on its path to economic prosperity.

*Peace, freedom and prosperity*

Zambia as a country may boast to offer peace and some freedom. Currently Zambia does not offer prosperity—genuine prosperity. So Zambians leave and choose to live abroad where they find peace, freedom and prosperity. They use the peace and freedom to prosper. And as they prosper they share their prosperity with families back home in Zambia. Most Zambians I know, including myself, send money home to support siblings through school. They also support their parents and other relatives. These are families that otherwise would be destitute if they had no one outside Zambia. The Zambian presidency should take time to account for this support, which comes from individual Zambians outside to their families in Zambia. If a president cannot see this, perhaps he needs another degree and an economics or commerce degree this time. Possibly ask Western Union why it is so successful in Zambia.

## The Children's Future

At the heart of every Zambian's consideration to live outside Zambia is the future of the children. What kids learn, see and do as they grow up becomes their culture and tradition. I am afraid that the current culture developing in Zambia is not a culture future Zambia will be proud of. What would you be if all you see around you are mishanga boys, refuse, intolerance, poverty, etc? I bet you grow thinking that is normal life. So there is no urge to move away from that way of life.

Most Zambians love their children. So when they have the opportunity to raise them in a decent environment, they would rather do that than in Zambia. They guard the children's future. What future is the current Zambian leadership promising Zambian children? It's time to start doing the right things.

Zambians being abroad has nothing to do with them being incompetent and inefficient. Rather it is a reaction to a system that is perhaps reckless, self-serving, uncaring, deceiving and perhaps not trustworthy. The challenge facing Zambian leaders is not to call Zambians back to Zambia. Rather it is to demonstrate that you have integrity, are trustworthy, wise, and honest; are fair, reliable, truly democratic, tolerant and caring. If you do the right things Zambians both at home and abroad will see and if they choose, they will stay or return.

Therefore, rather than forget completely about Zambians abroad, I would advise that the president dedicate lines of communication—e-mail, phone and fax—with Zambians abroad. Zambians abroad will not only offer you ideas, but also encourage and motivate you to lead Zambia wisely to ensure sustainable economic development and prosperity. Zambia "in the sun" is home. TwCN.

# Two Hundred Fifty Million of Government Dollars Recklessly Spent! Who Cares?

T he government of Canada, under the leadership of Liberals, authorized expenditures to the tune of $250 million allegedly to increase the profile of the Canadian Government or is it the Canadian flag in the Province of Quebec. Why should anyone care? After all we live in this rich and peaceful country.

Oh no! Every Canadian knows how hard it is to generate a dollar. If you work as a telemarketer making about $7 an hour, perhaps you know that you cannot even pose on the phone without a supervisor eye balling you. So you work so hard and you are a taxpayer. If you are a professional making well over $40,000, you know how high your income tax is on your pay slip. If you are a shopper, you know how much Goods and Services Tax (GST) and Provincial Sales Tax (PST) can dig into your pocket. And if you just immigrated to Canada, you know you just spent about $2000 in processing and medical fees. And for someone to think they have the liberty to anyhow blow two hundred fifty million dollars from government coffers without accounting for it is nearly insane. This is hard earned money. I feel as if all my tax dues were gabbed up in those cheques to Quebec false advertisers or are they Liberal friends. For sure I care, and I hope someone must pay a price for this kind of reckless expenditures.

As someone relatively new to Canada, someone has negatively affected my trust. I thought I was now far from corruption on some continent, but it appears corruption is here too. What are Canadian values and who shall teach me these values? Who shall I trust?

Did I hear you say I can still trust Paul Martin? I am told he was the finance minister at the time the scandal took place. Moreover, Paul claims he did not have a smooth relationship with the former prime minister and his "indunas." But I would think that Paul still had a job to do. And if he knew his job better, he should have heard the noise of the wind. Maybe he had no power to stop it because it was in the jurisdiction of another minister. Should I buy that? That doesn't matter to me. And I know there is a Cabinet where I suppose fiscal matters are discussed.

History shows that when a government has no credible challengers, it governs until it destroys itself. And this is often a result of complaisance. As the saying goes, "a house divided cannot stand." So it appears the Liberal Party governed Canada to the point of self-destruction. First, it was the Chrétien versus the Martin camp. And it was during this divide that Quebec advertisers and few Federal government crown corporations were milking the government through fictitious contracts. And there was no one focused enough to notice the problem. Once one camp is dead, now there is room and time to see the problems. Second, are the so-called Quebec liberals versus the rest of Canada liberals? I find it sickening. I thought a liberal is a liberal regardless of where they live in Canada.

By the way, are there true liberals in reality? My understanding of Party loyalty is adherence to the principles of the party. But now we see someone or some people hopping from one party to another. You wonder whether this is a search for employment or is it a change in principles? I thought one does not change principles anyhow.

It appears Paul Martin is determined to punish the individuals who were involved as well as to ensure the recklessly spent money is recovered. As a taxpayer, I hope it happens. But will the Liberals be punished? This is what Liberals fear most. The polls show their popularity plummeting fast. If the rate of plummeting increases, they may find themselves with little support at the polls sometime this year.

The only hope Liberals appear to have is that the real opposition is still sorting out its leadership. The Progressive Conservatives would be ready if they had a leader. If I were in their shoes I would declare a sleepless period until the leader is elected.

I wish the NDP were actually sharp. They appear to have their house in order, but they are not actively seeking nor do they look prepared to form a federal government. This is an opportune time for them to really shine.

Last time around, the Liberals were an organized camp with a Red Book full of policies, though some were not implemented when they assumed government. And when the PC polls plummeted with Campbell at the helm, the Liberals were sure of victory and went around waving the red book. I wish the PCs and the NDP would have blue and orange books respectively. Because in as much as I am angered by what the Liberals have done to my tax dollars, I feel squeezed to the wall, but the only exit I can see appears to be the liberal exit. Shall the PCs come rescue me? Where is your house or are you coming for me? Please I need your help.

As for Paul Martin, I feel sorry for him. He just came in full of energy and enthusiasm to rejuvenate every Canadian. But the first order of business has angered him so much. I wish him a quick relief from his anger. He should keep on encouraging the liberals around him to put on brave faces. There is no real enemy out there other than liberals themselves. Martin should take it easy, perhaps the Chrétien style, and just do his work. He recovers my tax dollars, he might have my support, but I dare not guarantee it. TwCN.

# "Celebrating Growth and Learning"

I couldn't help it, but think about it over and over until I felt I had assimilated the intent behind the words "Celebrating Growth and Learning." By the way this is the theme that Umunna Youth Association of Manitoba chose for their recently held workshop (Feb 21, 2004). I had the privilege of being invited to speak at the workshop. I am so grateful to the organizers.

I am convinced that it took some intellect to come up with this theme. I cannot help it but commend the minds behind it. I also praise the Ummuna youth as well as their parents for taking the time to celebrate growth and learning. It is a notion well forgotten by many particularly in societies where child upbringing is regarded as not a community responsibility.

The youths of today face a myriad of challenges. Challenges that include completing school, selecting careers, making informed decisions, being involved in relationships, being involved in politics and community activities; and respecting adults, etc. Because of these challenges many youths go for the easy way out—whatever is cool with their peers. But I believe this can change. Adults bridging the gap through such workshops as "celebrating growth and learning" can change it. Workshops provide opportunity for dialogue allowing wisdom to flow from those who have the experience to those who are in a position to learn.

Any stage in life is critical to one's future success. Read on the surface growth means change from childhood to adolescent hood and into adulthood. But to youths who seek meaning in life, growth may mean successfully completing high school or college and/or university education. Growth may also mean a change in attitude. Developing positive attitude towards life's challenges and getting ready to tackle them. Growth may also mean taking on more responsibility. Responsibility towards family, work and/or community.

Along with growth goes learning. Learning is not only through school, but through life's experiences as well. Learning is also achieved by observing others, how they think, what they do and their aspirations. By learning we grow, and by growing we learn.

Growth and learning never end in one's life. Therefore, everyone must realize that they need to continually grow and learn. This realization puts life's challenges in perspective. For youths who take time to celebrate learning, it is indicative of their quest to develop into intelligent, responsible, trustworthy, respectful and goal achieving adults. It is from such youths that the leaders of tomorrow will emerge.

Every parent whose youth stands out and poses to celebrate growth and learning must be proud. For such youth will grow into adulthood enlightened and ready to tackle life's challenges head on. Celebrating growth and learning is an opportunity for youth to hear the wisdom of adults, and therefore be ready to use the same wisdom when challenges that demand it appear. Youths also have the opportunity to spend time together doing something critical to their development into successful adults in life. As well, youths have the opportunity to become aware of what they need to do to achieve their goals in life.

Celebrating growth and learning also provides opportunity for adults and youths, parents and children to bridge the gap. Utilizing expertise and professionals to provide youths information critical to their growth, success and prosperity. How many youths under the sun have such an opportunity? Very few. And because many youths don't have opportunities to learn in an encouraging environment, they either learn by costly mistakes, or learn late in life. And information received so late in life may not be of much use.

Given the opportunity to recommend an activity for youths, I would definitely recommend that other community groups should emulate what the Umunna youths did as well. Does someone think that getting youths out to an event such as this one is not easy? You may be right. In the beginning, yes it may be hard. But as more of such events are held and the benefits are shared by the youths to the youths, more will realize that they are missing something. One day they will want to be involved.

The African Community is especially endowed with talented individuals. Somehow there must be a forum through which such individuals as business professionals, professors, doctors, financial planners, accountants, etc. can share there expertise with young people. By so doing young people will be inspired and motivated to achieve more in their lives.

Canada is a land of opportunity. And those who learn about these opportunities early in life grow to successfully exploit them and prosper. Those who learn about these opportunities can as well be African Community youths. It may be challenging to mobilize youths and have them come out. But remember that charity begins at home. If we can teach the youths to dream and show them how to work to achieve their dreams, they will learn very quickly and will be happy to come out and get involved.

Anything that has to do with youths is worthy pursuing. As the saying goes, "the trees that grow are the forest." Therefore, the youths that grow are the community and are the country. Celebrating growth and learning at a time such as this is indeed timely. TwCN.

# Building an African Community with a Prosperous Future

T he African Community must be thankful to Mayor Glen Murray, who remembered there is need for the African Centre when the Sudan Relief and Rehabilitation Program, led by Akim Kambamba, approached him and the other two levels of government for financial assistance. Our brothers from Sudan approached the Mayor with a good plan and good intentions, and with all honesty addressing their dire need for office space. But Mayor Glen Murray suggested to them to not only consider their interests but the interests of the Manitoba African Community as a whole. Mr. Kambamba and his colleagues welcomed the suggestion and embarked on expanding the scope of their need to include the African Community. For this we should all be grateful to the Sudanese community.

In my conversations with Mr. Kambamba, I discovered that he is a very understanding and professional person with advanced interpersonal skills and ability to work with anyone with an open mind. Most of the outbursts following his call for a meeting of African Community leaders came about as a result of people not knowing and understanding the man who was spearheading the whole initiative. I applaud him for his calmness and experience with dealing with his brothers. He calls all of us brothers and sisters and I have no doubt he means it.

Now it is time for the African Community to rally behind the man, or whichever committee will be constituted, to pursue the dream of building the African Centre. To this end I would like to take the opportunity and provide a historic perspective of the African Community in Manitoba. I don't claim that the account is perfect, but I present it in the way I have come to understand it through the years I have devoted my time and talents serving everyone in the community.

## Multiculturalism in Canada

Canada is one unique country that promotes diversity of peoples and cultures. As such one of Canada's core values is multiculturalism and people diversity.

Winnipeg is one of Canadian cities, which boasts of vibrant cultural diversity. This is especially evident during its most famous and popular annual Folklorama cultural activity, which showcases the diverse cultures and peoples that make up the cultural mosaic of Winnipeg and Manitoba. Yet just a sample of the Canadian multicultural diversity.

Canada's dedication to multiculturalism encourages every group of people to identify and maintain their cultural identities and proudly share them with other Canadians. The result is a rich Canadian cultural mosaic of which Canadians of African heritages are a significant part.

## The African Community in Manitoba

Prior to 1980, all one could see of Africans in Winnipeg was one here and another there. No exact figures are provided. But it is likely that there were fewer than a thousand Africans in the province of Manitoba prior to 1980. In the 1980s, however, the number of African immigrants in Winnipeg started to increase. As the number of African immigrants increased, so did the need to be well organized.

In 1983, the African Association of Manitoba was formed. The only organized groups then were Africans from Nigeria, Ghana and Sierra Leone. The African Association of Manitoba served as a uniting organization of all the Africans who were settling in Winnipeg.

As different Africans arrived from different African countries they started forming their own associations. This gave rise to the idea of forming a Council of African Organizations in Manitoba Inc. (CAOMI). The Council of African Organizations in Manitoba was formed to unite different organizations. The organization of this council was spearheaded by Dr. Charles Olweny.

In 1997, one member of our community, Mr. Hamza Mbabaali, came up with the idea of having a Folklorama African Pavilion. Prior to that some of our children participated in the Afro-Caribbean Pavilion. But this did not provide opportunity to profile African culture prominently. They were merely tagging on our culture.

So in 1997 African Communities of Manitoba (Africa Pavilion) Inc. was organized spearheaded by individuals from Nigeria, Ghana, Uganda, Umunna, Democratic Republic of the Congo and Zambia. The focus of the organization was to organize the Africa Pavilion during the popular annual Folklorama cultural festival organized by the Folk Arts Council of Winnipeg. The performance of the Africa Pavilion proved to be a resounding success as many members of the community identified with cultural performances and experienced in Winnipeg the taste of home away from home.

The mission of the African Communities of Manitoba (Africa Pavilion) Inc. was to *"organize, manage and operate the Africa Pavilion during Folklorama; and establish the Africa Centre for culture, education and learning."*

Since 1997, the African Communities of Manitoba, Inc. has operated the Africa Pavilion so successfully that most African groups and individuals are now involved. This has resulted in greater variety of cultural performances, but has also necessitated the need for premises where Africans can maintain and display their cultural heritage to the satisfaction of all Canadians and visitors.

The African Communities of Manitoba Inc. is a registered not-for-profit organization. When it was initially registered a number of African Elders were asked to serve as incorporating Directors. But they left the operations of the organization in the hands of the younger people who could volunteer to serve as long as they were willing and able.

The prominent activity of the organization is the Africa Pavilion. The Africa Pavilion is run by a Steering or Coordinating Committee, which consists of leaders and/or representatives of various African organizations. The steering committee is open to any African community member who could volunteer to serve.

The Steering Committee approves the Chair of the sub-committees. The role of the chair of the African Pavilion Inc. is to ensure that the pavilion has a Coordinator and that various pavilion sub-committees are headed by different organizations. The Steering Committee ensures that ACOMI has a treasurer, who also serves as Finance Committee chair. In addition, the committee approves an Ombudsman for the African community who addresses any community misunderstandings. This way of managing ACOMI, however, has its own strengths and weaknesses.

*Strengths and Weaknesses*

The major strength of the way ACOMI is managed is that it is inclusive of all from Africa and everyone who has keen interest in the success of Africans here in Manitoba. It helps avoid conflicts resulting from wins and losses in elections. It also capitalizes on volunteer strengths—providing volunteer opportunities and allowing only people who are committed to serve.

One major weakness, however, is the lack of formal structure and a Constitution outlining how the organization should be run. The current structure is around the needs of the Africa Pavilion. Hence the reason so little gets done between one August and another. In as much as there are people who do different tasks, most of these are volunteers who serve the needs of the Africa Pavilion out of their own commitment to the cause. But this is not to say much cannot be done. What the community needs are similar volunteers whose only interest is pursuing the dream of building an African Centre just like there are those volunteers whose only interest is the Africa Pavilion. These volunteers must be part and parcel of the ACOMI Steering Committee.

I ask that you don't get me wrong here. Some situations are nobody's fault. I have been asked some really tough questions and I have not been able to provide ample answers. Some people ask me for bylaws and others have asked for the constitution. I don't have these at the Secretariat. All I have are the incorporation papers. Even the incorporation papers have the name of the organization as "African Communities of Manitoba (Africa Pavilion) Inc." I wish the Africa Pavilion in the name read "African Centre."

Therefore, in terms of structure, I would propose a very simple structure that speaks to the role of ACOMI, membership, the coordinating committee and appointment or election or approval of volunteer officers such as the Chair, Treasurer and Secretary from within the Steering Committee. The constitution should also speak to activities such as the Africa Pavilion and the Africa Centre. Such a structure would suffice for the needs of the African Community.

*The Future*

Now appears to be the time for the community to put its house in order. Time has come to address all outstanding issues. Time has come to look at the report and recommendations of the structure committee. There will be no opportune time like this ever.

It is important to keep in mind that when the Africa Centre is built, it will need to be sustained. That sustenance will be possible if all African communities unite and work together from the beginning.

Indeed "united we stand, divided we fall." Shall we all unite around the African Communities of Manitoba, Inc. and build a strong community with a prosperous future of which we all can be proud. TwCN.

# Kofi Atta Annan - An African Son Deserving Ovation

I trust that everyone knows that Kofi Atta Annan is from Ghana and is the seventh Secretary General of the United Nations Organization. His service at the UN has put him in the spotlight since 1996. He's been called "the rock star of international relations." And I enjoyed watching him on Canadian TV during his recent official visit to Canada. Being a son of Africa, he is a man who has overcome a myriad of challenges. Looking at his accomplishments, I believe Africans and everyone else can learn something from his leadership of the world's 191-nation member organization.

*Background*

Annan is the seventh secretary general of the UN, following predecessors Trygve Lie of Norway, Dag Hammarskjöld of Sweden, U Thant of Burma, Kurt Waldheim of Austria, and Javier Pérez de Cuéllar of Peru and Boutros Boutros-Ghali of Egypt. Annan began his five-year term on Jan. 1, 1997 and he was retained for the second five-year term in 2002.

Annan was born in Kumasi, Ghana, on April 8, 1938. He attended Mfantsipim Secondary School, an elite boarding high school in Ghana, from where I believe he learned to be responsible and developed some of his leadership skills he uses today.

It is reported that Annan once conducted a successful hunger strike to protest against the poor quality of food at the Mfantsipim school cafeteria. No wonder part of his goals at the UN is to eliminate poverty and hunger wherever it exists around the globe. Kofi Annan also got first hand lessons in politics and diplomacy earlier on from his family. Both of Annan's grandfathers and his uncle were tribal chiefs. Upon his retirement, Annan's father, was elected governor of Ghana's Asante province. In addition, in the early 1950s, while Annan was at Mfantsipim, Ghana was undergoing radical changes. Under the leadership of Kwame Nkrumah, a movement for independence was gaining ground and by 1957 Ghana had become the first British African colony to gain independence.

Like many Ghanaians, Annan attended the renowned University of Science and Technology at Kumasi, before proceeding on to Macalester College in St. Paul, Minnesota, USA., Institut des Haute Étude Internationale in Geneva, and the Massachusetts Institute of Technology, where he earned a master's degree in management.

Like most Africans in the diaspora who are gainfully employed rise through the ranks, Annan is no exception. He is the first secretary general to have worked his way to the top job through the ranks, being a 30-year UN veteran. His former U.N. jobs include personnel director, budget director, security coordinator and refugee agency executive. He served around the world, including postings in Ethiopia, Egypt, Switzerland and New York. Annan first gained international recognition during the Persian Gulf War, when he negotiated the release of U.N. staff in Iraq.

*Annan's leadership dream for the UN*

At the beginning of the millennium, three years after ascending to the UN's top post, Annan issued a millennium report entitled "We the Peoples: The Role of the United Nations in the 21st Century." This was, and still remains a remarkable document outlining Annan's vision as a leader of the UN. The goals in this report are called millennium goals and include reducing global poverty, improving education for boys and girls in poor countries, and relieving the scourge of HIV/AIDS. His strategy to tackling the world's challenging problems is building global community consensus. In this respect Annan seeks, without attacking specific regimes or individuals, to use the Office of the Secretary General as a vehicle for promoting values of tolerance, democracy, human rights and good governance that he believes are universal.

Thus far, Annan has proved to be an efficient administrator as well as world leader. He has not only saved the UN millions of dollars, but he has also been instrumental in convicing media magnet Ted Turner to contribute $1 billion to the UN.

Annan believes in putting people at the centre of everything the UN does. "No calling is more noble, and no responsibility greater, than that of enabling men, women and children, in cities and villages around the world, to make their lives better."—Kofi Annan.

*What others think of Annan*

Three years into his first term Barbra Crossette wrote in *The New York Times* in December 1999 that Annan has emerged as "one of the most provocative leaders the United Nations has known." Richard Holbrook, the former US ambassador to the UN, once called Annan a "diplomatic rock star."

Muhamed Sacirbey, Bosnia's ambassador to the United Nations, says about Annan, "People trust him because he is honest. He doesn't try to hide behind a false argument. He defends his positions on merit."

His own colleagues describe him as "self-confident and candid, with a keen sense of humor." Writing about Annan, Martin O'Malley & Ashish Dewan of *CBC Online* said, he "is regarded as a dignified, soft spoken gentleman, an idealist, and a man of compassion, tack and courage who inspires great loyalty among those who work for him."

*Lessons we all can learn from Annan*

Yes, Annan is an admirable figure. Africans must be proud of him. He has proven to the world that given a chance, professional Africans can deliver and they deliver well. My own take is that leading African communities wherever they are around the globe is like leading the United Nations of Africa. And those in leadership positions of their communities can indeed learn from Annan and possibly apply his qualities of leadership—visionary, goal oriented, tolerant, democratic, respecting individual rights, commitment to good governance, trustworthy, honest, self-confident, candid and humorous, dignified, idealist, compassionate, tactful, courageous, and ability to inspire great loyalty among followers.

Koffi Annan is the first world figure to visit Canada under Paul Martin's administration. And when he addressed the Canadian House of Commons, he received no less than ten ovations during his speech. Yes, Annan is deserving of those ovations.

*Behind every successful man there is a woman*

Annan is a busy man. Nevertheless, he has grown up children, a daughter, Ama, and a son, Kojo, from his first marriage to a Nigerian beauty. Being a diplomat, finding love internationally is no problem with Annan. He is currently married to Nane Lagergan of Sweden who once served as Legal Officer for the UN High Commissioner for Refugees. With the husband's annual income in the range of US$200,000 she can afford to be an artist and enjoy life in the official residence of the UN secretary general on East side of Manhattan in New York City. TwCN.

*Associate editor for this edition of TwCN is Juanita Desouza-Huletey.*

# African Community Leaders Demonstrate Passion for Unity and Prosperity

P assion for Unity and Prosperity appears as a tagline at the Manitoba African Community Secretariat (MACS). Behind it's meaning is a reflection of the quest of the African community. The quest for unity, results and prosperity. And given the opportunity to speak, community leaders and members express their deepest need for unity in no uncertain terms. This was evident in a recent community meeting addressing the Africa centre proposal (on March 13, 2004.) Not everyone had the opportunity to attend. So I thought I should do my part and share my take on the meeting with the rest of the community.

*Passion for Unity*

Africa is a vast continent consisting of over 50 countries. And her peoples are diverse with a multitude of languages. There is every reason for these people to be different from one another. But removed from the motherland Africa, Africans quickly realize that they need one another to be an effective group that can work to achieve better things – socially, culturally and economically.

In a multicultural society such as that in Canada, unity of community, if it can be achieved, is key to success and prosperity. This unity does not come about by chance. Individuals and groups have to take deliberate steps to achieve it. Everyone ought to realize that they are a significicat part to bringing about unity. This includes individuals, community and organizational leaders.

Despite the varied backgrounds, when Africans come together, you can see the quest for unity, results and prosperity. Achieving unity is, however, a challenge. It calls for people to put behind their differences which pose as a barrier to unity and progress. It calls for people to be patient with one another. Putting aside all ill feelings and striving for the common good. It calls for maturity of character, possession of a vision and ability to stand tall in the midst of animosity for those who lead. It calls for tolerance of one another's mistakes. It calls for forgiveness of one another.

At the meeting, it was not only pleasing, but a learning experience too to see our brothers from Sudan pass the test for unity. Rather than give up and throw in the towel, as perhaps many of us would do, they chose to stick in there and remain united and focused on the project with the community. Thinking about Mr. Akim Kambamba, the man championing the development of the proposal for the Africa centre, I can't help but to admire the man and join others commending him for his comitment to serving his "African brothers and sisters." His patience, his pleasant voice, his accommodating responses, his tolerance of dissenting views, his endurance of negative ideas was just marvelous. It reveals something more than just an African man. It reveals a man with unorthodox leadership qualities, a man with a purpose, and a man focused on making a difference in his community.

Beda Otwari, Secretary General of the Sudanese Association and SRRP member, was another impressive speaker. He stood up and declared "I forgive all who labeled us as renegades and opportunists." He underscored that the project in question is infact an African community initiative and not a Sudanese project. Hats off to these gentlemen.

If, as a community, we are seeking financial support from the three levels of government, this is what they would definitely like to see. A united community that has been tested in matters of unity and passed the test – Can you work together? Can you accommodate one another? Can you serve one another? Can you prosper as a community? Do you have credible leadership? Be glad, the answer to these questions is a resounding "Yes."

*Looking for Results*

Results breed prosperity. As a community whose quest is to leave a legacy for children, members must be willing to lay aside their differences and rally behind whoever emerges as a champion of a good cause. This was done before at the inception of the Africa Pavilion when our brother Hamza Mbabaali of the Ugandan Canadian Association of Manitoba (UCAM) championed the folklorama initiative. And it must be done now at the inception of the Africa centre initiative.

During the meeting, one individual after another commended Akim Kambamba and his colleagues of the Sudanese Relief and Rehabilitation Program (SRRP), for preparing the Africa centre proposal. Each individual underscored the need to unite behind them and positively pursue the Africa centre initiative. Most importantly, everyone appeared eager to support whoever would produce results. Seeing how far Akim and his group had come, and how near, so to say, it is to achieving the goal, majority of those in attendance chose to be part of the team that is promising results. Experience is the best teacher. And all know that mere talk does not produce results. It's action that causes change, that produces results that people are looking for.

In the case where egos are bruised there is need to give it a second thought especially when the opportunity to move forward presents itself. "Yes, at first my ego was bruised, but on second thought, I thought this was an opportunity to move forward," said Mwaka Kaonga (Zambia). Others thought competition is good. And if it works to the extent of producing results, we all must be for it.

What about the African Communities of Manitoba Inc (ACOMI) efforts of the past eight years? Shall we forget about the past? Far from it. What is happening is just an indication of the fact that the community is full of talented individuals. And they all need opportunities to contribute something to the community. There is so much that need to be done to fulfill community needs and yield prosperity. Given that we are all volunteers, one organization such as ACOMI may not have the time and resources to fulfill all existing needs. Therefore, as new blood is infused and new ideas and energies introduced, existing organizations must welcome such initiatives. With new blood, ideas and energies, there is momentum to move forward. As an umbrella organization, ACOMI must be accommodating and supportive of all progressive initiatives.

*Building a Centre for Children*

Why should we put behind our differences? Why should we rally behind the Champion? Why should we support the initiative? Many attending the meeting concurred with Muhoza Hakizimana, Executive Director for International African Child Relief & Peace Foundation of Canada, who said "because we want to build a centre for our children."

Children will look at the African Centre and remember their ancestors. They will know there is a history to their existence in Winnipeg. They will have a place to experience African culture. They will have a place where they can dance, sing, play and belong. They will have a place to meet with friends. As a community of children they will have a home.

How passionate are you for African community unity and prosperity? What will you do from today to help bring the African centre into reality? You can choose to partcipate, encourage, donate money, raise money or just be there and watch. And I hope you choose to be part of it. TwCN.

# Behind Federal Government's Budget Lines

T his week, Ralph Goodale, Minister of Finance, tabled the federal government's 2004 annual budget. For those who understand public finance and fiscal policy it is exciting time. I for one always enjoy taking responsibility, privilege and opportunity to read and understand the budget, and especially how it affects me as a minority, middle class professional as well as a family person.

*Background*

Generally, each level of government – municipal, provincial and federal – has well defined responsibilities. The federal government takes major responsibility for matters that affect all of Canada including defence, foreign policy, immigration and citizenship and the environment.

Provincial and territorial governments are responsible for such matters as education, health care and highways. They share responsibilities with the federal government in some areas such as health, agriculture and highways.

Municipal governments of each city or community are responsible for matters such as policing, firefighting, snow removal and recycling programs.

The degree of significance of each of the areas of government responsibility depends and varies with the jurisdiction and its citizens.

*What is a Budget?*

At any level of government, the budget is a blueprint for how the government wants to set the annual economic agenda. The budget document sets out where and how the government plans to collect and invest it's revenues popularly referred to as 'taxpayers money.'

At the federal level in particular, the budget provides answers to such questions as How much money will go to pay down the debt? How much to health care? How much to research and development? Will taxes go up or down? Plus other questions depending on priorities.

Where the money goes to support each level of government areas of responsibility depends on the government of the day's priorities and policies in place. Budgets are up to allocating money to priority areas. Priorities are areas that the government has identified as needing advancement or improvement or development. The government sets objectives, policies or guidelines to ensure that money is spent on the identified priority areas.

Often, government leaders consult with citizens to identify priority areas. As an individual citizen, if you wish to provide input into the budget, feel free to write your member of parliament or legislature or the minister of finance and advise on where you think you would like to see the government spending money. It is always good to do this about three months before the end of year, or when you hear that the government is conducting consultations on the budget.

*The 2004 budget objectives*

In it's 2004 budget, the federal government says the budget has two objectives. First, providing Canadians with responsible and prudent financial management; and second, taking the first steps to implement the vision presented in the speech from the throne of strengthening Canada's social foundations, building a 21$^{st}$ Century economy and restoring Canada to a place of pride and influence in the world.

To fulfill government objectives, this year's federal budget includes measures on responsible and prudent financial management, health, learning, communities, knowledge and commercialization, and Canada's relationships to the world.

One observation is that the first objective is not new. When John Manley, in his capacity as Deputy Prime Minister and Minister of Finance, presented the 2003 budget, he included as one of the objectives to "build the economy Canadians need by promoting productivity and innovation while staying *fiscally prudent*."

There is no problem borrowing this objective and including it in the current budget. But most importantly this objective commands more attention now because of the recent revelations about hundreds of million dollars scandal of government expenditures on adverstising in Quebec. And more importantly, rather than just having it on paper, the Liberal government, headed by Paul Martin, has taken measures to ensure prudent financial management.

Health is always part of the picture. But this year it is of utmost priority as a result of the Prime Minister having met with provincial Premiers. Although it is the area of highest priority it is being given an additional $2 billion as a one time injection. This money is additional to the $34.8 billion provided under the 2003 Health Accord.

*What's new?*

Learning entered the picture as a result of high cost of education in Canadian univerisities. Most importantly this is where we find something totally new, that is, the Canada Learning Bond (CLB) of up to $2000 (over 15 years) for every child born after 2003 in a family that is entitled to the National Child Benefit (NCB) supplement. Also, we see an introduction of a new upfront grant of up to $3000 for first year post secondary dependent students from low income families, that is families with a combined household income less that $35,000. New minority arrivals, perhaps including those from Africa, may benefit from this support. But those who are professionals should not count on it.

The budget also includes money for communities. The major communities that will benefit from this year's budget are cities who will receive GST relief to the tune of $7 billion over a period of ten years.

One good piece of news is the $15 million that will be allocated annually for enhanced language training to reduce labour market barriers faced by skilled immigrants. The most beneficiaries are those immigrants who come from non-English and non-French speaking countries of South America and Asia. Few from Africa who wish to learn English or French may benefit as well.

Just how does this budget benefit smaller minority communities such as the African community? There is nothing specifically targeted towards smaller minority communities. To see the benefits you have to see the minority communities as part of the main stream Canadian society. Minority communities benefit through health care. Those who are residents benefit through learning as well. Organized associations benefit as there is some funds set aside to support the community based non-profit sector. The challenge is knowing how to access these funds.

As part of the main stream Canadian society, members of minority communities benefit from the fact that the budget is balanced. A balanced budget ensures the government is not spending money it doesn't have. This prevents deficits. If there were a deficit the government would be forced to borrow money. Government borrowing drives up the cost of borrowing, that is, interest rates, which in turn affect everyone's borrowing ability.

Moreover, the government is predicting surpluses which will help the government maintain its annual $3 billion contigency reserve. The idea of a contigency reserve is a very sound one. The contingency reserve is used to offset the cost of unforeseen events such as the 2003's SARS, BSE, BC fires, Ontario blackout and Nova Scotia's Juan hurricane. In the event that there are no unforeseen circumstances the government can use the money to reduce government debt.

It is comforting to see that the government has taken care of most of the victims of the 2003's unforeseen events. This is great as it shows, from among many reasons, one reason why governments are there. Well demonstrated - to help citizen's when they are in dire need. If the government did not have a contigency reserve, it would perhaps borrow.

Apart from the $250 million and $50 million financial commitments earmarked for missions in Afghanistan and Haiti, respectively, the government has also committed $248 million to providing international assistance. Much of Canadian international assistance is provided through the Canadian International Development Agency (CIDA) which supports projects in various parts of the globe including Africa.

Overall, this year's Liberal budget is very much a walk in the middle road. There is nothing on the right. But there is a little trickle on the left. Individuals, especially middle-class professionals, living in Manitoba may be pleased that there is no increase in taxes. The best, of course, would have been to see a tax break. But not until we see the new PC party's policy paper it is difficult to tell whether this is possible with the current leadership.

*Dream for the Canadian economy*

Governments, like individuals, have dreams and wish to achieve their dreams. Last year, the Canadian economy was forecast to grow at 3.2 percent. But because of the unforeseen events earlier alluded to, Canada's achieved economic growth was down to 1.7 percent. In 2004, the economy is forecast to grow at 2.7 percent. But this is just a dream assuming that the Liberals will still be managing the economy.

In case of a government change, the dream for the Canadian economy may also change. Hence, priorities, policies and objectives may change. But most importantly, regardless of who is running the government, do you know what the existing or new government should do for you? What is your dream for Canada? Please have the courage to share it. TwCN.

# Barriers to Success

Once upon a time some pioneer immigrants came to this country. After finding themselves in a land of opportunities, freedom, wealth, and much space, they decided to call it their land. Furthermore, they appropriated for themselves the exclusive right to decide who joins them in their adopted land. They marginalized the indigenous people, limited their opportunities and created a society in which indigenous people would feel unaccepted.

When growing economy and the demand for qualified labor force necessitated opening the door for new immigrants, these pioneer immigrants put in place discriminatory immigration policies that favored those from Europe over anyone from other regions of the world. Perhaps they didn't know any better. And they may have argued, who wouldn't do the same?

According to David J. Hall, "It was under Clifford Sifton's guidance that Canada adopted an aggressive immigration policy aimed at populating the West. In order to attract as many settlers as possible, Sifton established colonial offices throughout Britain, as well as in many European countries and in the United States."

Hundreds of thousands of new settlers arrived from the British Isles and from Eastern and Central Europe. These emigrants formed the social fabric that was the basis for the European cultural diversity found in the Western provinces today. The pro-European immigration policy worked. Hence today, Canada's population is predominantly Europeans. Other races are in the minority.

With the increase in population and a growing economy, the need for an efficient and effective transportation network system arose. The government decided to build a national railway system that cut across the country. For this, the government needed laborers. The Japanese were allowed into Canada to supply the needed labor to build the railway line. They were however, not accorded Canadian citizenship. So when the Second World War broke out and Japan fought against the Allied Forces, many immigrant Japanese in Canada were either repatriated back to their homelands or sent to detention camps. The Government of Canada recently admitted and apologized for its misguided actions against Japanese immigrants during that period.

The Government advertisement asking for people to immigrate to Canada targeted Europeans and restricted immigrants from other countries. For instance, the Chinese who tried to immigrate to Canada were charged a head-tax, which in all respects was somewhat equivalent to today's exorbitant immigration application fees.

In those days, the only people of African decent allowed in Canada were those who fled from the bondage of slavery in the United States in the late 19th century. They arrived in Eastern Canada and were not necessarily welcome with open arms. Some of them died and were buried in unmarked graves. Those who survived were marginalized socially, politically and economically.

It was not until the sixties and later seventies that immigration policy changed to make Canada a welcoming place for people from all parts of the world. And so today, contemporary Africans have migrated to Canada in some-what reasonable numbers. These new African immigrants, together with the ones before them continue to face barriers, visible and invisible to success.

Barriers to success, especially for people of African heritage, come in many ways. Firstly, there are people who migrated from Africa to this land in search of opportunities for personal success, good education, employment and a good life. They came here expecting no problem in establishing themselves. But this expectation is often far fetched, when they experience hardships with respect to finding gainful employment.

Secondly, for those today who want to migrate to Canada, the majority of whom are innocent, genuine, law abiding and decent people and some of whom have families in this country, one barrier is that immigration officers have so much power that even if you qualify, if the officer does not like you (because of whatever reason: - accent or face, or your shape, or your height) you can be refused migration into Canada. If you demand to know why you are refused, you may consider yourself luck if you are given a reason.

To the ordinary person, this appears to be normal business. The officer has done his job. And that may be fine. What is most bothersome is the fact that if you had the money, you could engage lawyers and ask them to fight teeth and nail for you, and chances are you could be allowed into Canada. This is true for quite a number of immigrants into Canada.

The "ecstasy" news comes to mind at this point. And the people involved may be just a tip of the iceberg. Such people deal in ilegal activities and accumulate so much wealth. They have the ability to bring anyone they want into Canada especially when the criteria for entering Canada involve showing how much money they have.

Could it be that the policy in favor of those who flash dollars above an average person is actually a barrier? Can it actually deny the good citizens opportunities, and favor potential criminals? Has this policy shattered the dreams of many decent people and instead has fostered accomplishments of those who are potentially problems? I trust you are a better judge than I am.

Thirdly, even if you find yourself in this land where your dreams are supposed to be fulfilled, you may find barriers to opportunities. When you speak in terms of professional careers, what comes to mind at the onset are traditional professions of law, accounting and medicine. In the past it was rare to find people of African heritage in these professions. Nowadays, things have changed though just a little bit. Accounting has made inroads to a greater extent and has minority professionals in gainful employment. Law has made inroads to some extent and has a few minority professionals in practice. Medicine has a good number of minority professionals, but most of them have stories to tell. Generally, those who find themselves practicing these professions do not have an easy ride. Most are subjected to unnecessary scrutiny.

Those who received their education before coming here are subjected to re-examination, re-certification, refresher training, etc. Those who are here are subjected to admission exams and interviews. Exams are no problem. After all, Africans like competitive exams as long as they are done in good faith. But the problem is that exams are barriers with a bias to limit admission of minorities. And exams are not an end in themselves.

If you do well in your exams you still have to do well in the personal interview. The personal interview! Yes, the interview, which is meant to assess your suitability for the profession. Just in case you didn't know, there are two requirements namely, qualifications and suitability for the profession.

Unfortunately, if you are from outside, a minority for that matter, chances are you are most likely to be deemed unsuitable. I have seen young people of African and Middle East decent denied opportunities for medical careers. I have seen their dreams shattered. I consider this kind of treatment adversarial to people's career growth and success. It destroys people's will, drive and passion for success. One can only imagine the torment that people who fail to achieve their dreams go through.

How did these barriers come about anyway? Could it be that there have been some 'bad eggs' in the past? And so all coming along must prove themselves. Or could it be that someone recognized that these are lucrative professions, and therefore, must be protected so that only sons and daughters of a privileged class must get into them? These are profound questions to which answers are worth finding.

For those planning to go to school, one way you can beat the system is not to put all your eggs in one basket. If you have opportunity to go to school, consider a double major or a major and a minor. If you are already a professional, consider professional development in another field.

Areas to consider for second major or professional development include, for example, specialized knowledge in project management, quality management, communications, etc. If you did this, and the unfortunate happens so that your dream to practice your profession is not achieved, you can spread your 'tentacles' and utilize transferable skills within a broad range of industries if not within your industry.

Another attempt at beating the system is to have the few who are already in there to demonstrate unparalleled professionalism in their practices. This means strictly adhering to the Code of Ethics and living professional lives of integrity. Continually serving with enthusiasm and building a professional image that reflects focus, the pursuit of excellence and admirable performance in the practice.

Finally, as I always like to end, the barriers existing today are a challenge. But my dream is one day they will go just as Europe favored immigration policies ended. My hope today is to live looking out for champion leaders who will not only be committed, but work to remove these barriers once and for all. TwCN.

*Following the preceding edition of TwCN which highlighted Barriers to Success, I received positive comments from some readers. In my continued research on the topic, I came across a piece of scholarly work by Dr. KC Prince Asagwara. Upon consulting with him he permitted that I bring you for this follow-up edition of Barriers to Success an excerpt of his work.*

# Immigration: The Professional Group

*Contributed by Dr. KC Prince Asagwara*

Before the 1960's, Canada's immigration policy was restricted and in favour of whites. In fact, Canada and Australia were the only Commonwealth countries whose immigration policies advocated whites only. In the early 1960's, pressure began to mount for immigration reforms.

Following the introduction of the Charter of Human Rights, the U.N. began to put pressure on Canada to open wider its immigration door to people of all races without discrimination. The newly independent African governments and other Third World leaders criticized racial restriction at Commonwealth meetings, and Canada acknowledged the need for changes in its immigration policy. During this period, Prime Minister John Diefenbaker had declared that Canada rejected discrimination based on race, national origin, colour, religion or sex. He introduced in the Parliament a Bill of Rights which was passed in 1960.

The Bill made changes in the immigration policy inevitable, and in 1962, revised immigration regulations were released. Section 31 of the new immigration regulations emphasized education, training, and skills as the major factors for admission into Canada. What this meant was that intended immigrants who meet the above criteria would be considered on their own merit without regard to racial origin.

Another contributing factor to the change in Canada's immigration regulation in the 1960's was the demand by employers for more skilled immigrants, and politicians who represented ridings where large ethnic voters were concerned with discriminatory immigration regulations.

Following the changes in immigration regulations, skilled and professional people from the Commonwealth countries of Africa, India, Hong Kong and West Indies became eligible to migrate, and most who applied to come to Canada had better skills than the usual applicants from traditional European sources.

In 1966, greater changes were recommended in a government White Paper which called for an increased immigration within the non-discriminatory parameters of 1962. The amended immigration regulations became effective in 1967 and introduced a "point system" which approximated the now skill-oriented immigration policies to specific value in the various criteria such as education, age, health, language, and work prospects.

The changes in immigration regulations benefited many young, skilled and educated Africans who had studied and acquired various expertise in Europe and did not wish to return to their homes in Africa immediately. Many migrated to Canada and a good number of them ended up in Manitoba.

It is a shared human characteristic to always want a better life. Economic and social advancement were motivating factors in the decision of these Africans to migrate to Canada. Most arrived with the expectation that they will accumulate wealth within a reasonable short time, return to their homes in Africa with their acquisitions and establish a comfortable life. In the pattern of the student group and characteristic of the African attachment to their ancestral homes, only very few of them are committed at the time of their arrival to make Canada their permanent home.

The Canada which those African professionals came to is friendlier and more welcoming than the earlier generation. The idea that immigrants who are not from Europe or of European stock are not knowledgeable and skilled enough to be accepted into Canada was giving way to acceptance based on one's own merit and equal status. In addition, the 1960's and 1970's, during which most of the African professionals migrated, the Canadian economy was in peak and in need of the qualities possessed by the Africans. But, despite the improvement in attitude and a booming economy, most Africans have been disappointed in their dreams.

The exception has been medical doctors from Western European universities, particularly Great Britain. Almost all have suffered from non-recognition of certificates and qualifications. Most have had to accept jobs where their skills and knowledge are not fully utilized. Trained engineers have had to work as technicians, a good number of them had to go back to school to improve upon their skills, and those who seem to have found a niche in their professions are put in dead-end positions.

*Excerpt from: "A Profile Of The African Community In Manitoba," by Dr. KC Prince Asagwara.*

# Me! A Leader?

In November of 2003, I had the opportunity to meet Linton Sellen, President & CEO of Training Plus, a Winnipeg based consulting firm. During my encounter with Linton I had the opportunity to engage in a rich discussion focusing primarily on leadership. Linton's impression on me ran deep. Partly because he made me recognize that ordinary people like me can be leaders and likely we are in a number of ways.

Everyone can be leader. And we are all leaders. Perhaps you are already asking "Me! a leader?" Yes, we are all leaders. But what is different about each of us is whether or not we are indeed effective leaders.

Often leadership is applied in a limited sense to organizations or workplaces. The truth, however, is if we all understood leadership, we would recognize that we are all leaders and as such we all must share leadership responsibilities. Much of this depends on the context, however.

This edition of TwCN serves to help you become aware of your leadership opportunities and roles in your workplace, community and even at home. Most importantly, as you become aware of your leadership roles, you will also realize that you are a significant part in building a community of effective leaders. Why? Because leaders are always in the process of making things happen and you want to be part of that process.

## What is leadership all about?

Most people confuse leadership and management. The two are different. Whereas management deals with things, leadership deals with people. Managers don't need to be leaders, but leaders must definitely be managers. Managers are called so because they manage processes, systems, methodologies which use or combine with other resources to produce some results, outcome, product or services. Leaders are called so because they lead people. And leaders must be concerned with the performance and well-being of the people they lead. Often in school, be it advanced or elementary, management skills are emphasized more than leadership skills. And this is why in many cases people assign leadership responsibilities to wrong people.

## A leader's job

Quite often leaders would have a vision and a plan of where they wish to take the people they are leading. These people could be a nation, a workgroup, an association, an organization or even a family. In order to move towards achieving the vision effective leaders basically perform five functions (1) Select (2) Communicate (3) Train or develop (4) Manage (5) Motivate. The challenge is always finding a leader who possesses the ability to perform all these five functions. Most leaders are good and are often chosen based on one or two abilities to fulfill these functions.

Since leadership is about dealing with people, who often are equals or subordinates, effective leaders select people with whom to work; people who would help achieve their vision. Effective leaders also communicate with people what they need or wish to see done. If the people don't know or lack some abilities, effective leaders train these people or develop them to a level necessary to achieve the vision. Effective leaders also manage people and other tasks within their span of control. That is, they plan, direct, organize, coordinate and control the work. In order to ensure there is enough momentum to accomplish goals, effective leaders motivate people to work.

If a leader does not perform any of these five functions chances are something will be left undone. As a chain is as strong as its weakest link, so is effective leadership. Often subordinates don't distinguish these functions. They would generally say one is not a good leader based on the failure to fulfill one or more leadership functions. So it is a challenge for leaders to possess all the abilities and qualities that would enable them to perform these functions. And awareness of these functions is one step to being an effective leader. Aren't you happy that now you know? I trust you are.

*Leadership styles*

Several terms are used in the literature to describe leadership styles. I am sure you have heard of such terms as autocratic, authoritarian, democratic and laisez-faire styles of leadership. I would not encourage you to use these terms when you are describing yourself as a leader. Instead try using action words such as directing instead of autocratic, coaching instead of authoritarian, supporting instead of democratic and delegating instead of laisez-faire. Needless to say that most people are aware of democratic leadership, so this can be used interchangeably with supporting without any misunderstanding.

Adopting action words accommodates and allows a leader to assume different leadership styles depending on the situation, issue or circumstances. Most importantly, leadership style depends on one's skills, competence, experience, personality and emotional state. This is why self-control or self-discipline is a critical virtue every leader must possess.

*Qualities of great leaders*

Regardless of where you are leading, three attributes make for leadership – character, way of thinking or approach and technical knowledge and skills. Often you will hear that great leaders are charismatic, persuasive, good communicators, visionary, goal oriented, dynamic, great planners, make big impact and have technical expertise. But history shows that the world's famous dictatorial leaders all possessed these qualities. For example, Sadam, Hitler, Idi Amin, you name them, they all were called leaders. But would you really call them great? Probably not.

So how do you really know great leaders? In order to recognize great leaders, you must determine to see both hands of a leader. On one hand great leaders must possess the above listed qualities. On the other hand, great leaders also must possess such qualities as honesty, integrity, loyalty to their people, trustworthiness, looking to the best interest of the people they lead, unselfish, good judgement, self-control, self-discipline, humility and courageousness.

How many of the leaders you have known have a balanced possession of these qualities? What about looking for them next time around? Finding good leaders can be a challenge. Often you don't know if someone is a good leader until you have the opportunity to see them lead, and especially lead you.

*Leading under stress*

The common experience any leader will tell you about is likely stress. And if you want to know if you are a leader, just look out for the amount of stress in you. This is true because leadership comes with responsibilities. The process of fulfilling those responsibilities yields stress. How a leader handles stress defines whether they are an effective leader or not. In addition to their own stress, leaders must handle their subordinates' stress as well.

When people are stressed, leaders must play a special role. If you are leading when enxiety is high, be calm. If you are leading when stress is high, try by all means to be less stressed. A leader must always play as the counterbalancing agent.

*What's in for you?*

Again this edition of TwCN serves to help you the reader recognize that you can be and are a leader. Being aware of the roles, functions and responsibilities of leadership and the styles you can use to lead in different circumstances – at work, community and at home must help you become an effective leader.

Often we hear of the expression "community leaders." Yes, community leaders can be effective leaders by selecting who they want to work with, they can communicate with each other and community members the goals of their leadership. Community leaders can train or develop others into being good community members. As well, community leaders can and do manage the tasks and affairs of their organizations. Community leaders can also motivate members of their communities to be active and to contribute positively to the well-being of the community.

Most importantly, each one of us is a leader. You and I can select or can be a factor in selecting who we want to work with – workers, associates, teammates, colleagues and staff. We can communicate what is important to be done; when we know and we notice others don't know, we can train them. And daily we have our own work tasks and time to manage. We can also motivate others to work positively, harder, smarter and achieve their goals. We can do this at our work places, in the community or in the family. TwCN.

# Well Disciplined To Excel

They work in light of negative perceptions. Reactively, they offer their very best, and now have a reputation of delivering exceptional quality work. Most of them went to school in their home countries, likely wearing school uniforms. Guess who these are? These are African professionals working both within corporate Canada as well as the three levels of government.

Their quest to achieve began while in primary school. When daily, in some schools, teachers on duty inspected their uniforms, nails, hair and teeth. In the process, even at that young age, most came to learn how to care for their uniforms, cut nails, comb their hair and brush their teeth. So they were disciplined and learned to be responsible at an early age.

When it came to academics, most endured and excelled in competitive exams. They had to pass with flying colors in order to continually attend school. They performed competitively in math, science, english, geography, social studies, and other subjects. When they left primary school, most attended boarding secondary schools. There, they learned to be responsible teenagers. Those who failed to learn how to be responsible had their failure reflected in their final school examination results. The fate was no chance to enter university. But those who entered university were the "cream of the crop."

When they left their countries to study abroad, most if not all excelled in their graduate studies to the amazement of their western professors. They early proved that, given equal opportunities, African students in western universities would graduate with flying colors. This came as a surprise to some professors. And they had to adjust, some with difficulty, their negative perceptions about African students. Those who had opportunity to work in Africa through international aid organizations were not surprised. They had an earlier experience of display of brilliance by African students wherever they taught in African universities.

Then it turned out that when these students decided to stay, and/or those in African universities, who had already received western university training, decided to come back and work in the West, they brought back with them their brilliance and excellence. At first, they experienced difficulty in finding gainful employment; not that they were not qualified, but the hiring parties were not just sure of the calibre of people they would hire. They had no experience working with such people and could not afford to gamble. But this kind of behaviour could not last in a free and democratic society of the West.

As Ralph Waldo Emerson, the nineteenth-century poet and essayist, wrote, "The world makes way for the person who knows where he or she is going," somehow, a courageous few decided to hire professionals of African decent. Some did it in response to the mandated affirmative action of the three levels of government. And as expected, the few that were hired delivered with brilliance excellent work. Most of these professionals became known for their hardwork, strong analytical abilities, excellent communication skills, willingness to work long hours, willingness to accept hard tasks, and ability to deliver excellent results.

These professionals have found their labour of love in their work. Despite having found their labour of love, most of these professionals continue to work against some negative perception on their abilities. So when they work, they work to prove themselves. In the process they deliver excellent results beyond expectations of their bosses. Unfortunately, for many this is where the road ends. This is what one African son, Dr. K.C. Prince Asagwara, refers to as "dead-end positions."

Often the boss is happy that the work is being done brilliantly. He or she is covered in terms of meeting quality requirements of work. His or her record looks great. And many such bosses use the excellent results to further their careers up the ladder.

Most African professionals, however, seek opportunity and not security, even though security is also important. Dr. Dennis Kimbro, author of *What Makes the Great Great: Strategies for Extra Ordinary Achievement* says, "The individual who knows where he or she is going and is determined to get there will find a way or create one." When African professionals hit the so called dead-end, it's about time to seek other opportunities, which include leadership and/ or managerial opportunities. Such oportunities may come within the same organization if it is large enough such as government, or by moving laterally to another organization at a higher level than currently held.

To this end, African professionals need to develop one special skill called *assertiveness*. Contrast that with aggression. Assertiveness, as defined by Ken and Kate Back in *Assertiveness at Work* (McGraw-Hill, 1982), is, "Standing up for your own rights in such a way that you do not violate another person's rights. Expressing your needs, wants, opinions, feelings, and beliefs in direct, honest, and appropriate ways."

Michael Armstrong, author of *Be An Even Better Manager* (Self-Counsel, 1990) says, "When you are being assertive you are not, therefore, being aggressive, which means violating or ignoring other people's rights in order to get your own way or dominate a situation. Assertiveness is about fighting your own corner. You have to believe in yourself and what you are doing and express your beliefs confidently and without hesitation." Therefore, your professionalism must positively influence others in your workplace.

One challenge for most African professionals is to remain competitive. In other words, to wear out, but not rust out. This is where professional development comes in. Should you find yourself in this situation, consider taking courses in leadership and/or management for your professional development and qualification for lateral and upward mobility.

I believe that African professionals are different. I have heard that even in United States of America, given the option between hiring African-Americans and Africans, American employers prefer to hire Africans. This is because Africans are different. And they demonstrate their difference in their dedication, discipline, focus and excellence in their work. One may argue that perhaps they are easy to satisfy with minimal compensation. Needless to say that when these African professionals are given entry level positions, they are minimally compensated within applicable pay scales. Often the situation is that of take it or leave it. Being offered the first job, who would leave it?

Onother challenge comes in distinguishing between African professionals and their kids born and brought up in the West. The kids perception of life seems to be totally different from the way their parents perceived it while in Africa. I should here say that most of the kids are very good. They are excellent kids. But also, many others appear to be problematic and, in certain instances, in trouble with the law. Some can't stay in school, and can't keep their jobs. It's most worrisome to say the least.

As the saying goes, "It is the bad eggs that spoil the whole lot." If this trend continues, it may be hard to maintain the reputation established by African professionals. And I am afraid that it may be as in America, where employers will prefer minorities from Africa rather than those from here. If that happened, some of the kids born of African professionals would not have such an optimistic future as their parents hope they should have.

This, perhaps, is an opportunity for African professionals to find time to contribute to their communities by volunteering, and putting in place programs, or providing services that will help to instill in young people African values of discipline, focus, dedication, achievement, and excellence. Here is Help Wanted! Would you be willing to take up the challenge and nurture the dream in young people? If you would, then step forward and do something. TwCN.

*Associate editor of this edition of TwCN is Vimbai Dune.*

# Destructive Challenges Confronting Our Youths

What is child's success? Martin Rossman, associate professor of family education at the University of Minnesota, partly defines child's success as quality relationships, finishing education, and getting started in a career. It is an excellent definition that probably every parent can live with. The dream of every parent is to raise successful children. And it is not as easily done as written down. But it is important to know, strive for and hopefully achieve.

Our children and youths may not fulfill their parents' dreams unless they avoid problems in which many of today's youths find themselves. This edition of TwCN focuses on identifying, or simply reaffirming, the four challenges or some destructive habits that confront young people, including our children.

*1. Alcohol*

I still remember when I was a kid, perhaps 12, and my parents, or some guardians, drank some home brewed "katata" drink. Often on a Saturday, when I was home, some of these older people offered me some alcohol to taste. And I remember I did taste it once. I didn't like the taste of it, let alone, its smell. From there on I refused to drink any alcohol, and to this day I never.

Looking back, I can only say I was the lucky one. Other kids, however, did taste. Although many like me did not like the taste, somehow, they embraced the habit even into their school years. Generally speaking, most of those who loved and took to alcohol at an early age did not grow into such successful adulthood as their parents may have dreamed for them. The habit of drinking alcohol overwhelmed many, at one time or another, during their early budding lives.

Yes, some people still argue, as long as you drink responsibly, you have no problem. This argument is best valid for adults and already responsible people. For a child or youth whose mind is so delicate, and who is just learning by sifting through bad and good habits, knowing and taking to alcohol at a young age is often a dangerous gamble.

Chances are young people who take to alcohol will also likely indulge in other illicit activities which will adversely affect their lives. If they are with smokers, when they drink they feel they should smoke. If they are with girls, when they drink they feel they must have sex. If they are driving, when they drink, they feel they must speed. These indulgencies breed problems in young people's lives that many adults are familiar with. Some of these problems may even include death at a budding age. Which parent would gladly witness this? Bet not one.

*2. Drugs*

In my time, I remember seeing some young, perhaps innocently unruly boys taking to drugs. These drugs included snuffing petro (or gas) and smoking. When I look back, I could say that it wasn't even a sophisticated society then. Fortunately, by virtue of the way I was brought up, I never partook in this habit nor did I have friends who did. Today, when I hear of drugs, I imagine they are speaking about varieties of drugs with varied effects on those who indulge in them.

Drugs are addictive. Youths who do drugs have a big problem. Youths who take drugs, have the desire to become high. Youths who are high do not do much in school or at work or at home.

Also, these drugs are expensive. Youths involved in drugs should be preoccupied with finding money with which to get these drugs. This preoccupation at such an early age is not necessary. At this age, youths are expected to be in school and focus much of their efforts on school work.

No youth can do drugs alone. Doing drugs calls one to be part of a group, often bad company. As the saying goes, "bad company corrupts morals." A company of young people involved in drugs is never productive. Such a company will indulge in illicit activities including drinking, smoking, sex, and often stealing. Again, no caring parent would be proud of such youths.

*3. Sex*

Given to man as a gift by the Creator, sex when indulged at the right time and with the right partner is thrilling and fulfilling. It's a gift and no design of man. But indulged in at a wrong time in one's life and/or with a wrong partner, it is perhaps the most destructive thriller. So young people who indulge in sex risk ruining their lives.

When the Creator gave man sex, He gave it with a blessing to enjoy, procreate and multiply the race. By design, procreation and multiplying the race comes with responsibility. And young people who choose to indulge in sex do themselves a disfavor.

Adolescence is a period of building a strong foundation for a brighter future, surprisingly including a happy and enjoyable loving marital relationship. So often young people take a leap at sex confusing it with love. Sex on its own and for its own sake is destructive and irresponsible. Love, on the other hand, does not only include sex, but also breeds happiness and responsibility. Ironically, much of happiness in a conjugal relationship comes from responsibility, that is, role playing, and not sex which is much craved for by some youths.

It is common understanding that young people are not prepared to take on responsibilities that come with having marital relationships. Therefore, young people who indulge in sex take a gamble at ruining their lives by calling on responsibility at a time they are not prepared for it.

Often, when youths bear a child, they cause on themselves and their child unwarranted suffering the effect of which many readers, I believe, are familiar with. As a teenage parent, a youth has no good education yet, and therefore, has no decent income. As a result, teenage parents have no means to fully support themselves and the child.

Some parents and teenagers may argue, if in fact this is arguable, that they can indulge as long as they are careful, not to get pregnant. Well, there are other dangers that come with experiencing sex at an early age. Once experienced, it's like alcohol, you want to have it every so often. But with who? Youths don't marry at that young age!

Also, often youths don't have the discipline to stick to one partner. So they have to move from partner to partner. In the process they risk picking up all kinds of sexually transmitted diseases (STDs). And evidently today, AIDs/HIV has claimed lives of millions of young people around the world. Most of whom learned to be promiscuous at a young age. Young people may find sex enjoyable and surprisingly thrilling, but there is a price to pay. And the desire that young girls must attract young men, and that young men must prove themselves are misplaced feelings. Reason and abstanence are likely the best bet for helping young people build themselves into responsible and successful adulthood.

Moreover, why does the law forbid poligamy? Research shows that those who never experienced sex before marriage succeed in their first marriages. Contrast that with those who experienced sex earlier in there adolecent years. These have no much regard for sticking to one partner in marriage. A good number involve themselves in extramarital relations, which often lead to broken marriages. Therefore, youths who choose to indulge in sex take a gamble on their future marriages, especially if they care enough.

It is said that knowledge is power. In order to raise youths successfully, parents and communities must face and discuss these challenges with their youths. And as the youths know they will be empowered to overcome these challenges and grow up to be successful and prosperous adults.

*4. Child abuse*

Often abused children grow into problem kids. Abuse comes in different forms and may include one or a combination of physical, verbal and emotional abuse. Much of abuse, but not all, is a parent's or guardian's responsibility. When abused children grow to become youths, they essentially protest against their parents or guardians. This protest takes the form of indulgence in destructive habits – alcohol, drugs and sex.

Few youths may be fortunate and realize the misdids of their parents and look out for a role model from somewhere else. Likely, a sports figure, teacher, or someone from within the family or community may serve as a role model. It is such young people that grow up and become great achievers and excellent role models in their communities. But they are very few.

Lastly, perhaps you realize that it took great courage on my part to come out as I did. I hold myself to higher standards and continually strive for excellence. Many youth programs today focus on therapy and rehabilitation of unfortunately already "spoiled" youths. But this often comes too late for most youths. The wise way to do it, I suppose, is to focus on prevention. And that calls for identifying root causes of problems and carefully finding effective solutions that help good youths not indulge in destructive habits. And the next edition of TwCN suggests solutions and ways to empower the youths to overcome these challenges. I hope then, I wont need as much courage. Whoo! TwCN.

# Empowering Kids To Be Responsible Youths - Part 1

I t's time to search for solutions to those destructive challenges confronting our youths. And as I suggested earlier, perhaps the best approach is long term preventive action.

It is important to realize that the world has no parenting schools. However, in lieu of parenting schools the world has families. And when all is said and done about troubled youths, everyone looks to the family to lay blame or find solutions. This underscores the significance of heads of families empowering kids to be responsible youths.

I am pleased to bring out this work. More importantly, the research I did helped me discover that I am no master parent. Being a parent of four children at the time of writing this edition of TwCN I felt as though I was setting myself up with a challenge – to bring up my kids successfully. Nevertheless, I am all thankful that I have had the opportunity to learn.

Many themes exist on empowering kids. But the underlying message of most, if not all the themes, is that the key to raising successful youths, those that will live to excel in school, home, or work is teaching *responsibility*. Probably this may not sound strange to many. But you might soon discover that the difference and the determining factor of whether or not you raise successful youths lies in how you understand and teach that responsibility.

*Chrispin Ntungo*

*What is responsibility?*

From the research conducted so far, I am most impressed by the writings of Beth Tucker, Virginia K. Molgaard and Kate Rice. Time and space would not allow me to simultaneously reveal and present other works by numerous writers. But effort will be made to bring out this valuable information in parts.

Answering the question, "Responsibility is the ability to recognize and react appropriately," says H. Stephen Glenn. Building on this definition, Beth Tucker of the University of Arizona in her article entitled, *"Building Responsibility: How do I teach my children to be more responsible?"* writes, "Responsibility is a value children learn from their parents, schools, peers, and society. It is a lifelong skill that helps children be successful throughout life. **Children grow into responsible adults when they are taught and guided to act responsibly.** Teaching your children responsibility can begin when they are young."

"Finding ways to teach your child a sense of responsibility is one of the best characteristics you can develop in your child. Research suggests that children *who are told what to do...not to try this or that* may grow up to have real difficulty making decisions. **Parent-guided** decision making helps children try out and learn responsibility. This is particularly important because "failure to learn responsibility is related to failure in school, in work, and relationships." "How?" you may ask. Because research shows that "children who act responsibly receive more *positive* attention from adults and peers." And as expected positive attention encourages positive response in children.

"Guiding your young child towards more responsible behavior can and should begin with 4 to 8 year olds. Parents ask: "How do I teach responsibility?" "Without realizing it, you're teaching your children responsibility, by your behavior and words. Remember how young children delight in pointing out your errors, such as saying a nasty word. They're learning through watching and repeating what they see you do," says Tucker.

The goal of many parents is to make it possible that at age 18 or so youths can live on their own and make responsible decisions. To a larger extent, whether or not a child will grow to be successful and fulfill the parent's goal depends on how they have learned to be responsible and make responsible decisions. This is where I found invariably useful the work of Virginia K. Molgaard, a family life specialist with the Social and Behavioral Research Center for Rural Health at Iowa State University of Science and Technology.

In her report entitled *"Teaching Responsibility to Preteens, Teens,"* Molgaard suggests four approaches to teaching responsibility, including gradually let go, long-term parenting, joint problem-solving and following through on agreements.

*Gradually let go approach.*

Molgaard says, "Parents do almost everything for their child during infancy. However the child gradually learns to do simple things-feeding oneself, walking, making needs known, learning how to dress, and so on. Parents usually are anxious for the baby and small child to do more and are proud of each new thing their child learns. It is easily forgotten, however, that preteens and teens also need to continue to do more things for themselves."

What is Molgaard getting at here? She is getting at teaching responsibility. "Parents who continue to solve their preteen's problems or make their decisions make it more difficult for their child to become a responsible adult. Unwanted parental control at this age has two possible outcomes, neither of which is healthy."

"Some children with controlling parents never learn to stand on their own two feet. Even as adults, they *cannot make decisions* and may *have trouble living away from home."* The inability of some youths to make decisions is what makes them prey to peer pressure or mob psychology. "Others react to excessive control by *becoming rebellious.* When they no longer live at home, they may behave in ways their parents had tried to prevent; they may use alcohol or drugs, engage in promiscuous sex or other dangerous behavior. On the other hand, parents who *gradually* let their child take responsibility and solve his or her own problems help prepare that child for adulthood."

*Chrispin Ntungo*

*Long-term parenting approach.*

Molgaard also says, "The kind of parenting that gets young people to do what you want in the short term doesn't usually teach long-term goals, such as responsibility and maturity. Short term parenting is characterized by:
- adult power and control;
- nagging and bossing;
- trying to prevent a child's mistakes;
- harsh punishment;
- insistence on "their" way, and
- a concern for, "What will other people think?"

"One problem of short-term parenting is that children and teens may do what parents want while they're watching, but go behind their parents' backs to do what they want when parents are not around."

"Long-term parenting takes time and may not appear to be working at first. However, young people gradually develop responsibility and the ability to think for themselves. Long-term parenting is recognized by:
- parents who share feelings with their children;
- help from children in setting rules and consequences and solving problems;
- helping young people learn from mistakes;
- respectful listening, and
- a concern with, "What will my children think about themselves?""

*Joint problem-solving approach.*

Molgaard says, "Young people can suggest possible solutions to any situation that causes trouble for their parents or themselves—household chores, homework, peers, schedules, even fighting with brothers and sisters. Joint problem-solving, in which parents involve their child to brainstorm solutions, is a good way to teach responsibility and how to make decisions. She suggests to use five steps:

1. Describe the problem
2. Tell how you feel about the situation (both parent and child)
3. Brainstorm possible solutions
4. Try a solution
5. Select a time to check back

It's important for parents to practice what they preach here and in all other cases. Your actions send messages. Match your behavior to what you are saying.

*Following through on agreements.*

Molgaard carefully points out that: "Unfortunately, the majority of teens will not always keep their end of a bargain, even though they may have had good intentions. It's a parent's responsibility to follow through with reminders about the agreement. If reminders don't help, the solution isn't working. Try another solution."

"The follow-up approach has a number of traps for parents," says Molgaard. "These traps include:
- the idea that parents and their children have the same priorities. Face it, youngsters usually don't usually care as much as parents about a clean house for instance. Instead, let your child know that you expect him or her to keep an agreement.
- a parent who criticizes, judges or calls names instead of focusing on the task. Comments such as, "How can you be so irresponsible!" and "You live like a pig!" don't help the situation. Parents can say, "Our agreement was that the vacuuming would be done by noon."
- not getting agreements in advance." Without advance agreement you have no reference point.

Lastly, as you can see the dream to raise a successful child requires thought and planning by parents. It is noble work for which all who have grown to be achievers must appreciate their parents. TwCN.

# Empowering Kids To Be Responsible Youths - Part 2

T his is our mission: finding solutions to destructive challenges confronting our youths. And I have laid grounds for focusing on finding preventive measures rather than therapy. In the first part of empowering kids to be responsible youths, I presented Molgaard's four approaches to teaching responsibility to preteens and teens. These approaches were gradually let go, long-term parenting, joint problem solving and following through on agreements. In this second part of empowering kids to be responsible youths, I plan to build on the first part and provide seven additional approaches or strategies.

*1. Use one word instead of a lecture*

In her report entitled *"Teaching Responsibility to Preteens, Teens,"* Molgaard further advises that parents should be tactful and sensitive to kid's way of doing things. For example, instead of lecturing, Molgaard suggests to simply use one word—"agreement" or "vacuuming" or "cleaning" to get kids going. Sometimes we as parents don't need to use words at all; a look, a smile, a raised eyebrow, or pointing to what needs to be done such as a coat dropped on the floor may be enough. As well, what we say and do must be appropriate to the age and maturity of the child and the situation. This requires us parents to develop a habit of putting some thought in whatever we say to our kids. As the saying goes "what you say does not matter, but how you say it."

## 2. Retain your dignity and respect

"Parents need to retain dignity and respect for themselves by following through, instead of giving up and letting a child do whatever he or she wants to do. At the same time, parents need to be respectful of the youngster, knowing that he or she will often resist. In some situations, it may help to write down the agreement, not as a threat but as a record," says Molgaard.

Should parents involve threats, or abuse kids verbally or physically to have kids do what they want? Probably not. Molgaard recommends that involvement of children in solving problems and providing parental follow through should never involve threats; and should never involve abuse either. The no threat or no abuse approach should allow parents to hold onto their power and respect, while letting their children keep theirs. It feels good for both parents and children and teaches cooperation and decision making. Hopefully, once parents get used to using long range parenting they can feel good about giving their children the best possible chance of becoming responsible, caring adults.

Kate Rice in a special to ABC News entitled *Raising Responsible Children, Believe It Or Not, Chores May Be The Best Technique* provides some experts' tips for raising responsible children.

## 5. Provide opportunity for positive risk taking

"As children get older, parents need to realize that teens are hard-wired to take risks," says Stephen Wallace, chairman of SADD (Students Against Destructive Decisions/Students Against Drunk Driving). But whatever the circumstances, "these risks don't need to involve alcohol, drugs or unsafe sex." Wallace observes "many parents consider that inevitable." And therein lies the problem. Parents giving up on providing direction. Many simply end up warning, "you will see when you grow up." He calls that the "myth of inevitability." He sees opportunities for positive risk taking. He suggests that "activities beyond the normal menu are most effective." Some of his examples include: "helping to build a library for children in Zimbabwe, mountain climbing, starting a community program for the homeless or getting involved in a project working with the elderly." It is such activities that build and produce role models from among youths.

## 3. Build a community of like-minded friends

"You don't have to do it alone, says James Morris, past president of the American Association for Marriage and Family Therapy (www. aamft.org) and assistant professor of marriage and the family at Texas Tech University. He considers the idea of two parents (or often even one) raising children alone is actually new and relatively unnatural. Anthropologically speaking, clans or extended families raised children, he says. So parents need to create their own little village for their children." This is particularly refreshing for people from Africa who believe in the saying that "it takes a village to raise a child." "That could be neighborhood friends, church or an informal group of like-minded families. At the very least, it means knowing your kids' friends and meeting their parents."

## 4. Make clear your expectations of responsible behavior

Parents should also be clear with children about what they expect from them. Often parents simply assume that kids will understand or somehow know or make the right choices, when in reality, parents haven't been specific enough. Generally, to make it easy for kids to understand or absorb instructions, a family should have a philosophy or a framework of how it does things as a team. Then, within the family framework of doing things, parents have to make it clear what it is that the children are responsible for. For example, you can have a family philosophy which says, "In our family we believe in taking care of our health. We believe in eating breakfast, lunch and supper. When it comes to school we believe in being first in school." Within that philosophy or framework you may ask your children to be responsible for remembering their lunch and/or their homework. And if a child forgets, perhaps it is an opportunity to let them feel the consequences, and hope that they will learn.

Kate Rice observes that having kids help with chores makes great sense on paper, but is often accompanied by such time-consuming resistance that parents end up doing it themselves. She advises to tackle it in increments. Give kids a chore list to check off. Start small with younger kids; add responsibilities as they get older. Or, if you're just introducing chores to older kids, add them incrementally. Remember the goal is to teach kids responsibility and to make them capable of doing chores.

*6. Give kids tools and show them how*

"Give them tools," says Rice. Set a time for cleaning rooms and/or making beds. Show the kids first how to clean a room or make a bed. Do it in a simple way by deconstructing tasks. This is important because children get just as overwhelmed by tasks as adults. For instance, a pile of toys can look overwhelming so help by giving them one toy and reminding them where it goes, start with the next, and so on. Another approach is trading off tasks. For example, promise a child you'll make their bed, if they put away their toys.

*7. Walk the talk*

Lastly but in no way the least, realizing that "example is the best teacher" is key to teaching kids to be responsible. As parents we've got to walk the talk ourselves. Let our philosophy always be to teach by example; accepting our responsibilities, being honest and working hard, trying to do what we say ourselves, and believing our kids will share our values.

Yes, the dream to bring up successful children is a beautiful dream. The challenge is it takes about half a generation to accomplish. And hopefully you are or will be committed to accomplishing it. Wishing you success. TwCN.

# Just What Kind of Parent Are You?

T hus far, we have looked closely at contemporary problems confronting our youths. We have examined some suggested preventive approaches to raising responsible kids. I am sure you agree that the subject is huge and there is no end to its discussion. The best we can do for now is at least, through TwCN, be aware of the problems. Hopefully we can apply the suggested preventive approaches to parenting and raise responsible youths.

As a last opportunity to bring out preventive solutions addressing the problems confronting our youths, I thought it worthwhile to consider one more important factor in all of this. The nature of parents, and therefore, of parenting. In short, what kind of parents are out there raising our kids? To answer this important question, I draw from the work of Dr. Daniel L. Baney, Ph.D. Psychologist HSPP of the Indiana Professional Psychological Services.

In his article entitled *"Raising Responsible Children,"* Dr. Baney identifies three distinct parenting styles or approaches related to raising responsible children: Punishing, Authoritative, and Indulgent. The characteristics, goals and results in children of these parenting styles are provided in accompanying tables at the end of Dr. Baney's article. You will notice, and perhaps most importantly, each of these parenting styles produces different results in children.

Dr. Baney points out that "**Punishing parents** tend to use punitive, escalating, and external pressure through grounding, spanking, "taking away", yelling, threatening - to try and control their children. Children respond by seeking power through rebellion, deception, and argumentativeness. Children refocus arguments on whether or not the parent is "fair", instead of examining whatever they did to invoke the punishment in the first place." As a bottom line, Dr. Baney underscores that "Punishing parents work *way too hard* in this power-struggle based approach."

"**Authoritative parents**, on the other hand," says Dr. Baney "are quietly confident in their parenting. They know children make mistakes and learn best by experiencing natural and logical consequences. They do not need to "invent" ever-escalating punishments, but, "allow the *consequences* to fit the crime." They give their children choices - so that the child can decide about their behavior - and therefore learn over time to make responsible choices." The bottom line, says Dr. Baney, is "authoritative parents guide, not control, their children by empowering them to make good choices and experience natural and logical consequences for poor choices."

Often the parent's slip is that they want it done now. They want obedience now. And the tendency is to punish in order to get what they want from the child. Putting oneself in the child's shoes, perhaps, will provide opportunity to do it the right way. But this requires awareness of what kind of parent you wish to be. And if it is to be an authoritative parent, then you need patience to become one.

Lastly, Dr. Baney identifies "**Indulgent parents** who seek to avoid the escalating conflicts and arguments characteristic of the punishing approach." Indulgent parents bail out the child often. "Here, *others* suffer from the child's poor choices as natural and logical consequences are removed. As the child is "bailed out" too often, the child fails to learn to connect "real world" consequences with their self-absorbed behaviors and choices and lacks empathy for the needs of others." The bottom line, says Dr. Baney, is that "others suffer the consequences of the child's poor choices and the child fails to grow."

Dr. Baney concludes that Punishing and Indulgent parents allow children to *externalize back to the parent* the primary responsibility for managing their behavior. Authoritative parents, on the other hand, tend to raise children who over time *internalize* responsibility for their choices and behavior. These children tend to grow up to be much more well adjusted, *responsible* and, therefore, happy.

Finally, Dr. Baney says, "I believe this to be true: **Show me a chronically irresponsible or under-responsible child, and I will show you an overly responsible parent who is likely frustrated or struggling to maintain control.**"

Probably, like Dr Baney you are rightfully asking, "What does this mean? How can a parent be overly responsible in today's world? Isn't this just another example of blaming the parent?" "Absolutely not!" says Dr. Baney, "It means there is a reciprocal relationship between parents and children regarding responsibility. If and when someone drops the ball or dirty sock, someone has to pick it up! It means we need to carefully look at what works and doesn't work in raising children to become responsible and dependable adults."

If your dream is to raise responsible children, then the challenge is teaching your kids to internalize responsibility and have the capability to make wise choices. To accomplish that dream, I guess you have discovered that you need to have a goal for your child. Then being aware of the implications of your parenting style, determine what kind of parent you ought to be to help your child fulfill your dream. TwCN.

# Election Time! One Opportunity for Networking

It is election time in Canada. And for those who live in Winnipeg, it is not only time to elect federal representatives, but also to elect a new Mayor for the City of Winnipeg.

What does election time mean anyway to minorities, especially those from Africa? After all, does it make a difference who is in power. Since whatever government is in power, one would suppose, is definitely better than the system left back home. As well, those who are new comers to Canada are perhaps not eligible to vote as they are not yet Canadians.

Moreover, life in Canada can be a struggle despite having decent homes or apartments and driving dent free cars. Some of those who are settled are continually struggling to pay bills, meet the demands of the family and have extra to send home. And some of those going to school are struggling with student fees, let alone student and/or immigration visas. Would election time mean anything to African minorities?

Fair enough, I would like to believe that election time means something to minorities and especially those from Africa. First, election time is a learning time. Those coming from developing democracies where every leader wants to be President rather than leader of the opposition, it is time to listen to leaders of different parties talk about issues and their platforms. And one lesson is that as they talk about issues they still respect each other's rights, including the right to live and the right to be covered by the press, whether that press is private or public. Then the people must decide whom to vote for based on the issues or platforms presented. There are no threats and there are no enemies made.

Secondly, and perhaps most important, as a minority group we can take election time as opportunity for networking. It is an opportunity to demonstrate that we are engaged in the democratic process. It is an opportunity to fulfill our dream to be visible to potential decision makers. The challenge, of course, is to get involved.

Elections Canada suggests that you can get involved directly or indirectly at any level you choose during an election. For those who wish to have power to determine who appears on the election ballot, you can join a political party. For those who just want to participate at election time, you can seek employment from Elections Canada to be a returning officer, or a ballot counter. Or you can choose to volunteer and help a candidate of your choice.

There are several ways you can get involved at grassroots level. Elections Canada suggests that the local constituency office is the best place to start. Candidates need people to answer the phone, solicit memberships, organize election campaigns, take part in rallies, open mail, and act as scrutineers. Also, you can visit a candidate's office and pick a brochure and/or a sign; put a sign of a candidate on your lawn; be visible, speak to a candidate and ask what they plan to do to improve minority opportunities for education, employment, immigration, or offer to help produce and distribute correspondence in your neighborhood.

You can also participate by being there on election day. You may do well if you choose a party and stick to it. But that is not necessary. Picking a candidate and rallying your support behind him or her is good enough. It doesn't matter whether you are eligible to vote or not. What is important is you helping minorities to be visible in the crowd. Your presence sends a message that you are part of Canada and you are a supporter of a candidate, you are involved.

Most importantly, as minorities, it does not matter whether the person we are supporting is elected or not. (If they are elected, good!) But what matters is that we have found a partner in the community. One who at the right time may stand with us and address or advocate our concerns. Therefore, pick a party and pick a candidate and offer to help.

I know Africans always want to be associated with winners. Supporting someone who does not eventually win may not sit well with some individuals. My take is that this is just another lesson. In some countries around the world, we see many who fail to win run to the bush because they don't accept defeat. I am glad Canada is different.

Look closely. You will notice on election day, that different candidates will be congratulating there opponents and will be promising to cooperate to enhance the ideals of Canada. This is an important lesson to many minorities who are new in Canada. Here people accept defeat gracefully. They pack their *election baggage* and continue with life.

So plan to do something that will make your group or community visible during this time of elections. And your involvement can be federal, provincial or civic, or all.

Lastly, I believe the dream to have our community visible is yours too, and that your challenge is how to get involved. Let this be your motivation and look forward to the accomplishment when you will get to know some people in the process whose friendship with you will continue long after election time is gone; and that what they see in you will reflect the spirit of the community. For that is the benefit of networking during election time. TwCN.

# Husband! Bring Out The Personal Best Out Of Her

WANTED! one most impressive, beautiful, intelligent and interesting woman. One woman who will travel the world, meet heads of state, dignitaries, participate in official charity and social events, appear on television, speak on a variety of topics, and get the education, experience and values to fulfill her career goals. One woman whose passions, humor and education will be fully cultivated. If you are interested, to be the successful woman you must beat at least 80 other contestants.

At least it intrigues my wife. It catches her attention. I can't get my wife to watch news or any sport with me. But when it is the Miss Universe event, she has the time and interest to be with me and watch. And if she is not available, I must be prepared to answer one or two questions.

Notwithstanding its seemingly exploitative potential, many share in the Miss Universe Organization's purpose to advance and support today's women. Women who are "savvy, goal oriented and aware." It seeks to "advance their careers, personal and humanitarian goals and as women who seek to improve the lives of others." The Miss Universe Organization "provides women the opportunities – the mentoring, career training, resources and life experiences. Women are personally enriched with year round support for all aspects of their lives, from their own personal career goals to social and humanitarian causes and work." Simply said, Miss Universe title holders personify the combination of beauty and intelligence that defines the 21$^{st}$ Century woman.

In return, the Miss Universe Organization is honored through the "personal bests" the women seek to achieve by cultivating their passions, humor and education. "We have a rich history of bringing together some of the most impressive, beautiful and interesting women from many backgrounds and cultures and then helping them achieve their goals" says Theresa A. Beyer, Vice President of Marketing for Miss Universe Organization. Through the Miss Universe telecasts "the organization celebrates tradition, while honoring the women, their talents and their hard work."

June 1, 2004 evening was the time. I could sense excitement, and delays in doing chores. First, I didn't know the reason, but passing my eyes across the TV set I saw unparalleled beauty. And I thought something good was showing. How could my wife's eyes be so focused. In quietness, I joined her. And the conversation ensued. "My friend called and told me about Miss Universe," said my wife. Knowing the history, I just made myself comfortable.

There are many aspects to Miss Universe, but I could only speak about what impressed me most - *National Costumes*. I could not appreciate any more than our own from the mother continent. Seeing them in gorgeous costumes would only remind me to be mindful of the sweethearts and darlings in my life, including my wife and my daughter.

I am not a kind of person that would sit and watch Miss Universe, if it were all left to myself. After all there is only a MISS universe. I had to find a way the event would be meaningful to me personally. I thought that perhaps every married man or husband would do well to think of a Mrs. Universe; and perhaps make his own to be the Mrs. Universe.

The Miss Universe title holder becomes a representative of the Miss Universe Organization, traveling the world, meeting heads of state, dignitaries, participating in official charity and social events, appearing on television, speaking on a variety of topics, and getting the education, experiences and values to fulfill her career goals.

Perhaps not all men would consider it wise to make their sweethearts travel around the world, or meet heads of state or dignitaries. Nevertheless, married men are reminded to help bring out the personal bests in their women by cultivating their passions, humor and education; honoring their beauty and intelligence, advancing their career goals, personal and humanitarian goals and partnering with them to improve the lives of others, including all in the family. TwCN.

# On Jan Lamprecht

There is nothing more humiliating than being powerless and paraded naked as we recently saw the American soldiers do to Iraq prisoners of war. Because of humiliating their men, most Iraqis are mad at Americans. Worse still, the humiliated victims themselves have scars that will remain with them their life time. Most felt it was better to be dead than to live.

The article by Jan Lamprecht, *"How black people struggle, the big lie about racial discrimination,"* on etherzone.com exposes some naked, and therefore, humiliating truths about black people. As a result, the first read of the article induces, in a black reader, an impulsive reaction extending to calling the writer racist or white supremacist. But such is an example of the impact of naked truth.

It would be one thing to throw medicinal mud into my face because I am handsome. That would be sheer jealousy. It would be quite another thing to throw medicinal mud into my face because I have leprosy. That would be healing. If Jan's article was written with honest intent to show black people their short-comings, it is worth reading for what it reveals. But if it was motivated by hatred toward black people, or if it was meant to serve racist and white supremacist propaganda, then it should be seen as a piece of thrash.

And don't misunderstand me, I am not in agreement with the entire content of Jan's piece. But Jan has said some truths that are not so easy to utter without being labeled racist. I take this exposure as particularly important in light of the way African societies and communities work. In African societies people respect elders, mothers and dads, uncles and aunties, elder brothers and sisters; and respect for its own sake is a good value. The problem is when respect precludes frankness, honesty or truthfulness. The good kids, boys and girls are those who agree with what the elders say, regardless of whether it's sensible or not. Because of that respect, blacks don't come out directly when they are sharing opinions. And this socialization impacts the way blacks deal with issues. Even when things are wrong or don't make sense, in many instances voicing contrary opinion makes you a rebel. This often allows poor conduct, bad manners and misbehaviors to continue in adults. This is even more the case with Africans in leadership positions. I am yet to meet an African leader at whatever level that takes kindly to criticisms. I appreciate the fact that Jan comes from a different culture, and was honest to say exactly how her people look at blacks. Wisdom tells me its good material to digest.

Put another way, what Jan said about black people are issues of responsibility, leadership, integrity, trust, hard work, love, care, peace and education. Jan is challenging blacks to be responsible. Jan is saying if black people could demonstrate responsibility, integrity, trust and practice what they learn in school – home, college or university – black societies would be better off. Yes, blacks do go to school. But does school change their hearts. Yes, they do have leaders, but are the leaders responsible, honest, do they care, or are they blatantly corrupt and tribalists?

Jan is challenging black people to prove themselves. If they are intelligent, let them do intelligent things. Yes, go to school, educate your children, but most importantly practice what you learn. Above all, demonstrate your intelligence in your communities and societies. Jan is perhaps appealing that the socialization of blacks ought to change. Jan draws a great deal out of history. And only history appears to be a good "barometer" for telling the successes and failures of people, including blacks. Jan is challenging all blacks to live honestly, to do honest daily work, be responsible in their homes, workplaces, communities, and everywhere they have the opportunity to shine, to shine indeed.

Jan speaks of black people being given equal opportunities, black people running businesses, black people being employed. How do black people take opportunities? How do black people run businesses? How do black people patronize fellow black people's businesses? How willing are black people to pay for products and services provided by black businesses? How do black people perform in their workplaces? Come on! Be honest, be courageous and face the truth. As the saying goes "know the truth and the truth shall set you free."

There are a few things black people can do to demonstrate that they are not failures; to demonstrate that they are in fact more intelligent than others. Try the following rules of personal conduct:

- If a steward – don't steal.
- If at work – perform your work with excellence, earn honestly your daily wage.
- If in leadership – lead with a good spirit, be honest, care for others, listen to everyone, don't kill the ones who oppose you.
- If in school – do your home work, be a reader, review your notes, study to get As.
- If it is broken – repair it.
- If it is in good condition – don't damage it.
- If it needs to be done – do it or find someone to do it.
- If paid a wage or salary – save for tomorrow.
- If poor – be prepared to work for someone so you can be paid, or do something, but don't steal.
- If rich – it's in your mind, help others whenever you can.
- If speaking – tell the truth, think before you talk.
- If teaching – teach clearly, and teach truth.
- If writing – write clearly, and be honest.
- If you are black – be proud, be happy, and smile.
- If you have an appointment – be on time, keep time.
- If you have kids – teach them values of achievement, work, care, responsibility, peace, respect, and love.
- If you promise – deliver on your promise, fulfill your promise.
- If you spill it – clean it.

Jan's view on intelligence can be regarded as racist because it is based on wobbly science. But for the sake of discussion it does not hurt to talk about it. And don't miss the point. Jan is not saying that every European or Asian person you see is more intelligent than black people. No, you don't even need to call on science to prove that is not true. There are millions of blacks who are more intelligent than many Europeans and Asians. Jan is speaking in collective terms. And as one of my friends likes to say, "white people have specialists in everything." It appears Jan is a specialist on black people achievements.

There are certain facts that are admirable in European and Asian communities. One thing I admire is the ability of Europeans and Asians to archive knowledge so future generations can benefit from and build on today's knowledge. I also, admire the European and Asian commitment to education. Intelligence is a function of education. In other words education and literacy are keys to increasing intelligence in people. And the mere fact that more Europeans and Asians than Africans are able to read and write, may make them appear to be more intelligent than blacks. Just as blacks that become equally educated and literate, appear to be more intelligent than other blacks.

Other factors of course affect black communities and somewhat diminish their success and achievements. Some of them are sheer jealousy, lack of drive and determination, inability to endure competition, unnecessary pride and show off, and the dependency syndrome. Should we continue to make the same mistakes that have hindered our collective progress or would this be the time to consider changing some aspects of the socialization process that seem to retard our development and advancement?

To sum up, yes, Jan has been blessed with her own frustrations. Jan's frustrations are, nevertheless, a challenge to black people especially Africans. Africans need to embrace something they seem to so much lack – courage to confront irresponsible leaders, challenge authority figures that fail to work for our collective interest and well being, build confidence that comes from conviction of purpose, and challenge adversity and overcome it. Whatever you label Jan, and whatever take you make of her frustration, now is the time to live the dream and prove her wrong. Would the "perfect" people of the world prove Jan wrong? TwCN.

# On Jan Lamprecht: Rejoinder

*By Isaac Katoyo*

No, there is more to Jan Lamprecht's article than meets the eye. It would not be alright to be dismissive. It is possible for one, even a group, to profit from the misery of others and hence call oneself intelligent, wealthy, etc. I categorically refuse to accept the notion that Africans are less intelligent in comparison with other races. The fact that some of our leaders have made mistakes, which have resulted in our continent lacking behind in terms of development is no cause for calling the whole of Africa as being less intelligent.

Those who stand to benefit the most from any exploitative, oppressive system have always sought to present themselves as pure intelligent and God sent messiahs.

When slavery reigned supreme, the ruler and the rich people of the day happily participated in this evil system and preached that it was the natural order of things. They saw nothing wrong in treating other human beings as animals and mere tools of production in the same way animals were treated then. During the slave trade, it was a religious belief that slavery was a God ordained form of society, that it was natural for the supposedly "superior races" to enslave the so called "inferior races." This is similar to Jan's notion, which is nicely camouflaged in a seemingly harmless article purporting to educate yet insulting. I am perturbed by her suggestion that Africans have a hereditary deficiency of intellect.

There is a lot of external propaganda and manipulation going on with regards to Africa's development. A case in mind is Zimbabwe.

You do not need to be a political scientist to recognize the class of exploiters, the capitalist class. This tiny class commands, controls and owns the means by which society produces the things needed in life. The greatest source of strength for this class is its inherent ability to turn the crisis it generates into causes for its existence. Those who owned the means of production in Zimbabwe together with there foreign supporters have chosen to ostracize the country without concern for the population, yet they call themselves Zimbabweans.

As regards our values there is totally nothing wrong with our values, and they are not the cause for Africa's underdevelopment, if anything our rich values cannot be compared with most of the western values. African values are traceable from the Bible, although Christianity was 'misused by say hypocrites' for colonial conquest, domination and exploitation of Africa.

Talking about Asia, there is acute poverty in India, North Korea and many other Asian countries; therefore to talk of Asians in Africa like they are kings and queens is unacceptable. Although not all of them, some Asians in Africa have been mentioned in some cases of money laundering and drugs. Some business have been closed because of the same.

Those who choose to come and live here in the Diaspora are free to do so, just like there are many white people who are crossing over into Africa some as individuals, families and as corporate institutions. The UK is still employing nurses from Africa, therefore its not a crime to come and live in the Diaspora and nobody needs to feel sorry for it.

The West and Europe continues to contribute to the degeneration of African economies. Take for instance Mobuto Sese Seko late President of the now Democratic Republic of the Congo (DRC), he is known to have stolen a lot of money from his country and I recall at one time he was known to have been the richest person in the world, he threw his country into abject poverty and left no infrastructure worthy talking about, yet he was protected and defended by the West and Europe. Look at what is happening in the DR Congo, that country is infiltrated by foreigners purporting to be Congolese supported by a Western power through a neighboring head of state. All because of its minerals. And so how do you develop in such instance.

In a letter published on 10 May 2004 in the British daily, The Guardian, the Swiss ambassador to the United Kingdom, Bruno

Spinner cites names of African leaders who have had money frozen in Swiss bank accounts. The question is why is it easy to freeze these accounts yet hard to pass on the money back to the countries involved. Institutions such as the World Bank and IMF have not helped matters at all. They have brought to Africa policies that have been detrimental to the development of Africa. Every prescription from these institutions serves interest of their donors (owners) rather than that of the people of Africa.

It is a pity and indeed a shame for her to claim that The Great Zimbabwe was built by Indians, like her forefathers who manipulated Africans and took away our land and destroyed most of the things that were achieved, she is trying to take way from an African anything and everything that will show creativity and intellect on the part of an African in order to advance her illusive notion. Indigenous Africans between AD 1250 and AD 1450 built The Great Zimbabwe, period.

"So when the strong conquer the weak and then bring to the weak a better system which enables the weak to progress and live better than they were able to by themselves is that not good?"

Who is she calling the weak? Is this what some people are calling advice? The many years of apartheid has given nothing good to the indigenous South Africans, the majority of whom live in the ghetto, are uneducated, unemployed and are facing a lot of social problems. The South African government is now faced with this mess left by the white government. You can see that this so called "better system," is there only to provide and secure the interest of "kith and kin" not the indigenous Africans.

She continues by saying "racial discrimination is nothing more than logic in action,"

Now let us agree that this statement is very painful to those who have and/or continue to experience discrimination. This is a mockery and negation of civility. TwCN-R.

# Why Black People Struggle - A Perspective

*By Dr. KC Prince Asagwara*

M ore than a week ago, I forwarded to you an article by Jan Lamprecht, a white South African apartheid apologist of the Boer ancestry on the above topic. I warned that at first reading, the initial reaction is likely to be that this article is racist and white supremacist. But a closer examination would reveal need for some individual and collective critical evaluation, analysis, and sharing of some home truths with each other on some of the contents of Jan Lamprecht's article. It was my opinion then that some of what are contained in Jan Lamprecht's commentary are essentially true though very inflammatory. I have read Jan's article three more times, that opinion has not changed. Rather it has added impetus to my urge to rejoin on this issue. Hence my rejoinder.

So far, two Africans commented briefly on Lamprecht's article and both took unbraid at Ms. Lamprecht and as expected, dismissed her as racist and white supremacist. I respect their points of view though I do not agree with them, not that Lamprecht may or may not be a racist and white supremacist but in the outright dismissal of all the issues she raised. As hard, painful, and inflammatory as some of the issues contained in Lamprecht's article may be, dismissing them outright and branding her racist and white supremacist is anti-intellectual and not academic. My view is that some of the issues raised by her have a ring of truth and calls for debate. Further more, feeling angry and dismissing Ms. Lamprecht as racist and white supremacist is analogous, in my opinion, to blacks in the US who routinely call themselves "nigger" and make light about it. But when a white man calls the black "nigger", the gloves come off. I hope I have not offended you by this analogy but, all the same, it has a ring of truth to it.

Bill Cosby, a notable black American educator, human rights activist, actor/comedian generally respected for his objective views on race and racial issues argued along some of the lines of Lamprecht's article less than two weeks ago. Although that he attracted opprobrium from some black leaders, he refused to back down because blacks sharing home truths with each other on issues of race and racial relations is over due. According to Cosby, instead of blacks in the US capitalizing on the myriad opportunities available to them, most spend their time in unproductive things, such as, buying designer this and that for themselves and their children, shun education, speak in trashy linguistic codes which will not open employment doors for them, refuse to be there for the kids when they need them most; and when those kids end up wearing the orange uniforms in county jails, we shout racism. Is there some truth here or not?

Our own Dr. Chrispin Ntungo as a feature of his "Thursday with Chrispin Ntungo" a week ago, opined that we should not dismiss Lamprecht's views on this issue, especially the salient points that call for critical self and collective evaluation and analysis. I read and found his take on some of the sensitive issues raised in Lamprecht's article useful and informing. I hereby take the issues both Dr. Ntungo and Lamprecht raised a step further. I have chosen to do this because providence has a way of being unkind to those men and women who enjoy the exceptional privilege of being witness to the truth but decide to take refuge in an attitude of passivity, indifference and sometimes of cold complicity. We can choose to bury our heads in the sand like the proverbial ostrich and live in denial. We can even engage in empty grand standing rather than confront the real problems of our very existence as a race. Ms. Lamprecht's questions are legitimate. The issues she raised are real.

Ms. Lamprecht wrote, *"...Black people rule more than 50 countries on this planet, and every one is a virtual disaster area..."*

What is there to quarrel with in the above assertion? Look at the carnage and destruction happening all over Africa. Last week, I forwarded to you a BBC News reportage captioned Congo rape victims seek solace. So far, it is estimated that the Congo war has killed three million people and involves armies from seven different countries. Women of all ages are gang-raped, mayhem and destruction is everywhere. Just imagine this, "They gang-raped me and pushed sticks up my vagina - that's when my baby died - they said it was better than killing me." Does this not bring tears to your eyes?

In Sierra Leone, the beat was the same. Africans chopped off the hands, legs, ears, gorged out the eyes etc. of their fellow Africans. Relate to this. "The rebels came into our house in the evening and took my 15-year-old sister away. My mother stayed up the whole night. The next day my uncle went from hut to hut looking for her. He called her name and heard her groaning inside a hut. He picked her up and carried her home. When my mum saw her she burst out crying. I was only 10 and didn't know anything about "man business". My sister was crying all the time and couldn't walk. She cried: "Oh mother, I'm going to die." My mother just held her and told her it would be OK. Similar atrocities took place in the Liberia war.

We all saw and were awed at the massacre that took place in Rwanda ten years ago - 1994. In Somali, everyone has ran amok, clans are killing and decimating one another. There is no rule of law; everywhere is in a state of nature. In Uganda, it was reported a week ago that Ugandans described as rebels massacred, and maimed thousands of their African brothers and sisters. Hundreds of women and girls are continuously raped. The Sudan war has consumed millions of African lives.

In Nigeria, if it is not religious killings, it is ethnic cleansing. People are routinely burned alive and buried in mass graves; survivors are deprived of their livelihood by fellow blacks and perpetrators are never arrested. Nigerians, since political independence, have killed more than 3 million of themselves. Is it not legitimate to ask how many Nigerian blacks did the white man kill during the period of colonial rule? At some point in the life of a people, there should develop a consciousness into self-discovery in order to move forward. Ms. Lamprecht in her article is telling us what we already know but refuse to admit.

Ms. Lamprecht wrote ... *"They are all mystified by the lack of black performance. They become frustrated because they see Golden opportunities thrown away. They see waste, they see corruption - and megalomania. They just don't understand the black psyche."*

If we want to be honest to ourselves, we will admit that collectively or institutionally speaking because that is what Jan is alluding to. When left to manage things for themselves, most African countries have fallen short of expectations. In fact, we (as in government and institutions) have ruined or ran down most of the infrastructures we inherited at independence. You see, when the colonialists were in charge of African countries, 80 per cent of national revenues collected were sent back to Europe. But what is more significant is that the 20 per cent left behind were well utilized in the establishment and maintenance of infrastructures. For instance, the few roads that were built, power and water supply, transportation system, education, health care system, etc. were solid, constantly serviced and well maintained. Today, all African countries control their economies as well as 100 per cent of the revenue derived. But in most African countries, you will hardly notice any evidence of this on the ground.

Go to a country like Nigeria and see what the black man has done with the railway system, which the white man under colonialism used the horsewhip to force our forefathers to build. When the colonialists managed our economy, Nigeria had steady supply of power, that is, electricity; water system was steady and efficient. Today, cities across Nigeria can stay days without electricity. Water supply is epileptic and unhealthy. Calculate how much damage the economy suffers as a result. How often has there been power failure here in the City of Winnipeg? Seldom, and for a few seconds, usually when there have been heavy down pour. Has any of us experienced shortage of water from your tap? I doubt it.

Nigeria is not alone in this inept collective, government, and institutional management of our resources. Everywhere in Africa is presently in a state of decay. Why? Because most of our African leaders and elite are common thieves and criminals in power who regard public treasury as their private estate. Remember that 500 years ago, African elite and leadership assisted the Europeans to sustain an evil system of slave trade that fed the greed of Western economic pursuit. Today things remain unchanged when you consider the looting and thieving of national treasuries by our leaders for deposits in European banks.

Let me provide you with a few instances you may already know. The late President Mobutu Sese Seko of the Congo stole and robbed his country blind to the tune of $7 billion dollars stashed away in European banks. The late Nigeria's military President, Sani Abacha reportedly stole and stashed into his European bank accounts more than $5 billion dollars. For the past four years, Nigeria's President Olusegun Obasanjo has been globe throttling to the Western countries asking for debt forgiveness without success. In one of the countries, he was reminded that if a handful of the scores of wealthy Nigerians whose wealth deposited in European banks were to repatriate their money, it would pay off Nigeria's external debt. Do not tell me that the West is to be blamed for the looting and thieving by the leadership of African countries because it is blame shifting and will not help us black people, if we are to get our houses in order.

According to Vanguard, Thursday, December 04, 2003 — Former British Secretary of State for Foreign and Commonwealth Affairs, Baroness Lynda Chalker, revealed that 40 per cent of wealth created in Africa is invested outside the continent. Speaking at the Private-Public Dialogue Roundtable on Business Partnership with NEPAD at the Commonwealth Business Forum in Abuja, she said that the story of African economies would have been different if wealth created in Africa were invested on the continent. She remarked, "If you can get your kith and kin to bring these funds back and have it invested in infrastructure, the economies of African countries would be much better than what they are today."

Tell me, is there any African country that is not ridden with crises, debt, mass unemployment, corrupt leadership, patricidal wars and refugees problems? Is it not our so-called leaders and elite that assists the neocolonialist and imperialistic multinational corporations in their greed to wreck havoc on our environment and exploit Africa's mineral resources for the enrichment of the West? Is it not in Africa and organizations managed by blacks that you see or hear of President for life? How often do you see a black person in leadership position relinquish that office without being pushed out or he killing those that want to take over from him? So let the white man spell it all out for us to see.

*Ms. Lamprecht wrote* "Look at the Asians and one will see among them the same ability to progress. De-colonization had actually been a good thing everywhere - EXCEPT IN AFRICA! …The Pacific and Asian countries, and even South America, had fared much better after decolonization than Africa had. What many people don't realize is that in economic terms, the African countries have gone backwards in proportion to what they were in colonial times. In terms of proportion, Africa has gone backwards for more than 40 years while Asian and other countries moved forward."

We have either read or heard about the so-called Asian tigers, which Ms. Lamprecht refers to above. They are South Korea, Taiwan, Malaysia, Singapore, etc. These Asian countries at Independence 40 years ago were as poor economically speaking as most African countries. In fact, poorer than a country like Nigeria. Malaysia for instance, came to Nigeria to acquire palm fruits for its palm oil industry. Today, Malaysia is the world's biggest producer of palm oil while Nigeria that used to export palm oil at the dawn of Independence now imports the same produce from Malaysia. In addition, these Asian countries have technologically advanced to the point of manufacturing cars and vehicles, including agricultural equipment.

Ms. Lamprecht wrote *"Japan, with no natural resources has the second strongest economy in the world, while Africa, which is up to its eyeballs in natural resources, and is potentially the richest continent in the world is actually the poorest."…There is a very real tendency for black people to live for today without a thought for tomorrow."*

In the above, Ms. Lamprecht is referring to the conspicuous consumption habit of African leaders and elite. It reminds me of a remark by Muhammad Ali that whenever you see a limousine or big Cadillac parked in front of a dilapidated building, the house likely belong to a black person. Around the world, every other race has pulled itself up by their bootstraps except the blacks. Blacks are busy looking for presidential jets, bulletproof cars, SUV, designer gears, etc.

About ten years ago, we saw 60 Minutes documentary on Malawi's President for life, the late Kamuzu Banda's state visit to Britain. President Banda with his entourage of family members, friends, government officials, sycophants and hanger-on went to Britain with hat in hand begging for financial aid. He received assistance in the tune of millions of pounds. We saw on the 60 Minutes documentary how 80 per cent of the money Banda received was used in purchasing then state of the art fleet of Mercedes Benz, Rolls Royce, Jaguar, TV/Video/Audio sets, fridge/freezers, Asian rugs in different colors and styles, electric cooking utensils of different varieties, in short, it was pure madness. As if that was not warped enough, Banda chartered a British plane to fly him, his entourage, and cargo back to Malawi. A Head of State who went to Britain for financial assistance in the name of Malawians virtually left behind in Britain 80 per cent of the financial assistance he received. What does that tell you about us black people as a race? Your answer is as good as mine. I believe this is one among the things that make blacks a laughing stock of other races.

Just imagine this. Nigeria's President Obasanjo has several jets in his presidential fleet. By contrast, the British Prime Minister does not have a single ministerial jet. He travels on commercial flight. The Prime Minister of Canada has no private jet either. He also travels on commercial jet. But when Nigeria's President Obasanjo and his coterie of Ministers travel, they stay in five star hotels in place of cheaper hotels, which would make more economic sense. Last year, Nigeria hosted the Commonwealth Summit, which cost several millions of dollars. Nigeria spent billions of Naira on importing scores of brand new BMW cars. A new hotel was built to host the visiting leaders. Furniture was imported from Italy and elsewhere for the event. What purpose did this extravaganza serve? None, except for Commonwealth Leaders to acknowledge Nigeria's President as an international statesman. I do not know of any white country whose leader would spend his country's over-spent treasury on a jamboree that is meant to give the toga of world statesman, especially, when his country has 45 per cent unemployment rate.

During the 1991 Gulf War, Nigeria derived an oil windfall profit of $2 billion dollars. The retired General Ibrahim Babaginda, Nigeria's evil genius was the President. The windfall of $2 billion dollars disappeared into private hands and has not been accounted for till today. IBB as Nigerians call him is today reputed to be one of Africa's wealthiest former Heads of State. Nigeria is the world's sixth largest producer of oil and the fourth in gas production. It has no functioning oil refinery at the moment. The three previously built have become derelict due to lack of maintenance. Yet Nigeria earns billions of dollars in oil revenue yearly. Most of the oil money rather than go into public treasury end up in private hands of a few elite. The end product is that a country that exports crude oil in commercial quantity imports refined oil at high cost. You do not need to be a brain surgeon or a rocket scientist to appreciate the havoc being wrecked on the economy, and the hardship that the average Nigerians endure.

I was in Nigeria not long ago. I found that 80 per cent of the asphalt roads have turned into death traps due to lack of maintenance. Most of the traffic lights installed in various and strategic junctions did not work either because they had broken down and could not be repaired or there was not power supply. Most of us drive on the streets and roads of Winnipeg. One of the rules in traffic regulation is that when you come to a two, three, or four way stop sign, whomever that stopped first has right of way. Most people observe this traffic rule. In Nigeria, you would be courting disaster or even death if you come to any of the above stated junctions on the street/road and stop. Someone is likely to run into you, and as well, yell at you for observing traffic regulation.

I could go on and on in the attempt to share some home truth with and amongst ourselves, blacks to reevaluate and critically analyze why we (government and institutionally speaking) do the things we do contrary to the norm and our peoples' best interest, and not because I agree with everything Ms. Lamprecht wrote about us or the racist and white supremacist tone implied. You will observe that I did not dwell on Ms. Lamprecht's point on the issue of black versus white intelligence and the role of DNA. This is because as she herself admitted, blacks at the individual levels are as intelligent as whites and Asians. Besides, there is no empirical evidence that any of the races is by DNA, more intelligent than the other in the absolute sense. There are varieties in the degree of intelligence amongst the races in both conceptual and abstract thoughts and reasoning. Ms. Lamprecht's suggestion that Indians or foreigners built the Zimbabwe Walls is simple manipulation and a non-issue.

115

In conclusion, my views here are not an invitation to a fight, verbal or written. You have the right to disagree with my perspective. I will respect it. Please do the same for me. You can also write to refute my points of view, and point out to me my errors. If you do this, it will be that you and I are singing the same song though in different tunes. TwCN.

# Reflecting on the Manitoba Election and Marathon

Once in a while everyone goes through some exciting times. The month of June 2004 will go down in my records as one such exciting time. It is exciting for me because of the provincial and City of Winnipeg by-elections, the federal government elections, Manitoba marathon, and being a soccer fun, the Euro 2004 tournament.

I would like to believe that the media does well and is good at covering public events such as the marathon, elections and sports. For this reason I am mindful of not repeating what most of you have already heard. Though the desire of some of you is to see me cover elections, a desire I appreciate, I however, choose to apply my principles and bring out what is not so obvious, yet very important in our lives.

Here is some of my attitude takings on the Manitoba election and marathon.

*Vandal's build bridges attitude*

There were nine major candidates in the city of Winnipeg mayoral by-election. All the candidates entered the race at different times relative to the nomination deadline. Some like Dan Vandal entered early, others like Sam Katz entered late, very late indeed. Vandal was a frontrunner from the beginning of the race. More so because he served as deputy mayor prior to his mayoral candidacy and had good understanding of the issues. He was very confident that he would finish the race a winner.

But Katz entered the race right on the last day of nominations. Being Winnipeg's Goldeyes baseball team owner, his name was widely recognized and he was mostly identified with those under 35. Because he was famous, he easily won the election with a landslide leaving Vandal in second place.

Most impressive was Vandals step to go to Katz's victory bash to congratulate him on his victory. "Sam Katz will be our next mayor. I know he is someone who will be a very good mayor, and the city will be well-served with him as mayor," said Vandal. These are truly gracious words coming from the mouth of a rival who has just suffered defeat. To me, Vandal demonstrated good leadership. Now here is my take: Vandal sought to build bridges. And just as Vandal built bridges with Katz, you and I could build bridges in many ways, including our communities, friends, families, workmates, and teammates.

*Katz's vision, hard work and determination*

Sam Katz may say he is not a politician. And he is right. But Katz is famous for winning battles. His accomplishments speak volumes about his attitude. Giving his victory speech Katz said, " Welcome to the beginning of a new Winnipeg. . . I know something about that kind of attitude. I have faced it before. I heard people say the Rolling Stones will never come to Winnipeg, a baseball team will never succeed in Winnipeg. With each of those projects, I brought vision, hard work, and determination and unwavering belief in you, the people of Winnipeg, and you never let me down." Patti Edgar of the Winnipeg Free Press summarized Katz's promise to his supporters as "a new kind of city, one that looks forward and does not pine for days gone past."

I believe you will agree that it is because of Katz's proven ability to have a vision and determination to work hard to achieve his vision that he was able to win the mayoral race. Commenting on Katz's win Jim Carr, president of the Manitoba Business Council, said Katz will bring "purpose, passion, commitment, energy and tenacity" to the mayoral function. And Chris Lorenc, president of the Manitoba Heavy Construction Association said, "Katz will bring a vibrancy and can do attitude to things that Winnipeggers will appreciate." Katz's attitude is an excellent attitude to emulate. Having a vision, believing in yourself, working hard and being determined to achieve your vision may be the key to your success.

This reminds me of Mwaka Kaonga, an accountant and a Zambian-Canadian single mother with six children under her roof. Kaonga ran in the twenty-six mile Manitoba marathon on June 20, 2004 just two days before the election. If you know anything about the marathon, you will appreciate the preparation that goes into getting fit enough to run a marathon. It takes vision and belief in yourself to stand up and do something for someone, to see yourself cross the finish line. It takes hard work to prepare, and it takes determination to finish the race.

Katz believes in himself and he believes he could do something great for Winnipeg. And Similarly, Kaonga believes in herself and believed she could do something for her children, family and anyone in need. But what is it that is so different about these visionaries and achievers? Winning an election, or finishing a marathon are just outside indications of the mental strength winners such as Katz and Kaonga have. It is their mental power that breeds a positive attitude and discipline to achieve what they set their minds to. This brings us to another take: like Katz and Kaonga, you and I could have that positive attitude and discipline to achieve our vision, our dreams, and whatever we set our minds on.

*Mihychuk's no quits attitude*

After the civic elections, there were those who lost. Of interest was MaryAnn Mihychuk, who I wanted to hear what she had to say. Mihychuk gambled big, leaving a comfortable position as minister of intergovernmental affairs in the Manitoba provincial government. "I am a fighter, not a quitter," said Mihychuk, who vowed to run in the next mayoral race in 2006. I thought this was a positive attitude too. Never to quit is perhaps too strong a promise since being an achiever demands some degree of wisdom. Most achievers I know are individuals who have the ability to assess the situation, or conditions, or circumstances, and determine their chances of success. And only when they see that there is fair play and opportunity to succeed do they go ahead and vow never to quit.

This reminds me of the Euro 2004 soccer game between German and the Czech Republic. German is renowned as a soccer powerhouse with four world cup and three euro cup championships. The Czech Republic played German after having won two games and being at the top of their group. However, they were determined never to give in to the Germans. Though the Czechs appeared to be under dogs, they believed in themselves. Despite German scoring first, when the game ended the Czech Republic had beaten German 2 goals to 1 and ended German's dream for Euro 2004 championship run.

Similarly, Kaonga run the Manitoba marathon with the same "no quit attitude." Speaking to Jullie Horbal of the Winnipeg Free Press, Kaonga said, "All I need to do is cross the finish line, whether it be walking or running." Kaonga's dream for personal success relative to the marathon was just crossing the finish line, which she accomplished. Her mental strength and determination to accomplish what she set her mind to may serve as a good lesson not only for her children but also for many who know, or just read about her.

*Kaonga's remember your roots attitude*

In the run of her life, Mwaka Kaonga was able to raise over $1,200 in individual donations for charity. And one thing she remembered to do was to remember her supporters at a moment that mattered most, even speaking to the Winnipeg Free Press. Kaonga said, "People at work, in the community, my friends and my neighbours have been great. I've also gotten tremendous support from the Winnipeg's African Community." I don't know what your take is on this one. But I thought she did an excellent job at remembering her roots.

It was news to learn that the Winnipeg mayor elect, Sam Katz's roots are in the North End of Winnipeg. I would suppose that this area must have been a flourishing area when Katz was growing up there. But given it's status today as an inner city, it's hard to believe that Katz grew up there. Today, Katz's residence is in Tuxedo, perhaps the richest area in Winnipeg.

Like Kaonga remembered her friends and people at work, in the community, neighbours and her own African community in her comments to the press, one would hope that Katz would remember his roots, and work to improve Winnipeg's North End and other areas of the city requiring tremendous improvement.

What's your take? I would like to believe that you and I have roots too. As we achieve our dreams and walk the path of success, shall we remember our roots. TwCN.

# Sudan: Too Much Talk, Little or Misplaced Action, No Improvement

Here is Alek Wek responding to CNN's Paula Zahn's interview questions. *"WEK: We have to step to the plate and really try and do something.*
*ZAHN: We know this is...*
*WEK: Excuse me. I get very emotional.*
*ZAHN: We can't possibly understand, having seen your family ravaged by this, but...*
*WEK: It's really hard. Because it's so simple. Something needs to be done. Once it's taken care of it, which it just needs to be the one main story and really follow it through. It does not need to be put aside." - Paula Zahn Now Wed. June 30, 2004.*

Likely, you are already asking, "Who is Alek Wek?" Alek Wek is a Sudanese who was discovered at an outdoor market in London, England in 1995, but has quickly become one of the hottest new sensations in modeling. She has overcome all the odds and successfully made it in the competitive world of modeling gracing international runways with her distinctly Sudanese beauty. Despite her success, Alek has not forgotten about her troubled homeland - Sudan.

Listening to her (Wednesday, June 30, 2004) during an interview with CNN's Paula Zahn, Alek's words, *". . . it just needs to be the one main story and really follow it through. It does not need to be put aside,"* resonated through my mind over and over. So I thought TwCN can do its part by adding one unique perspective to it. Of course, the story is true and is about the plight of the people in southern Sudan.

Like most people around the world dream of living in a democratic, peaceful and prosperous country, the people in southern Sudan have the same dreams. Unfortunately, southern Sudan has not seen nor experienced peace for the longest time all because it has long been wracked by a (supposed) civil war.

The June 30, 2004 edition of CNN.com reported, *"Human rights groups have decried an ethnic cleansing campaign in the region that has left between 15,000 and 30,000 dead and displaced more than a million -- with many of them fleeing to neighboring Chad. The groups have reported widespread raping, looting, pillaging, and the burnings of large areas."*

The Sudanese situation may be more complex that most of us outside Sudan understand it to be. Notwithstanding, TwCN learns that the situation in Sudan is such that the northern part of Sudan is predominantly Arab by race and Moslem by religion. The southern part of Sudan is predominantly black by race and Christian by religion. Overall christians make up 5 percent of the population, muslims 70 percent and the balance of 25 percent constitutes other faiths.

Also, the Sudanese government of Lt. Gen. Umar Hassan Ahmad al-Bashir is predominantly Arab and Muslim. And the war in Sudan between the north and south is not perpetuated by what one would obviously recognize as the Sudanese uniformed soldiers. Rather the war is perpetuated by Arab militias known as Janjaweed. The Janjaweed have continuously waged a campaign to expel black Sudanese from the vast and remote section of Southern Sudan. The Janjaweed are responsible for widespread raping, looting, pillaging, and burning of large areas including homes occupied by blacks in Southern Sudan.

It is at this point that one would ask where is the Sudanese government in all this? Why can't the Sudanese government protect the citizens of Sudan who live in the South? Good questions. And the fact is the government is there, but and unfortunately it is backing the Janjaweed, a fact it denies. Recognizing this fact, black Sudanese in

123

southern Sudan have organized themselves to resist the Janjaweed. The unfortunate thing, however, is that the predominantly black resistance movement is labeled "rebels" by the Sudanese government and from all media reports it seems like the international media concurs. Why is it that the international community cannot get it?

On Wednesday June 30, 2004, Paula Zahn of CNN also had the opportunity to interview Elie Wiesel, a Nobel Peace Prize winner and founder of the Elie Wiesel Foundation. Elie Wiesel, because of his work and direct involvement in humanitarian work, understands the plight of the black Sudanese people. Here is part of the interview:

*ZAHN: So you have as many as 30,000 people killed, more than a million people displaced. How has the world allowed this to happen?*

*WIESEL: Well, indifference is a disease, a contagious disease, seductive at times. And we have seen it in parts of the world occasionally that knows how to be indifferent. I wish I could change it.*

*But Sudan has become the world capital of human suffering, and not to be sensitive to that suffering is a mark of shame to all of us.*

*ZAHN: Do you think the world cares less because these victims are black?*

*WIESEL: I hope not. They are human beings.*

*But when we say the world, the world, of course, is a generalized concept. There are people who do care. For the last few years, people came to see me from Sudan and from Washington, actually discussing the situation and that I know that there are NGOs, there are humanists all over the world who do care.*

*But those in power, that's the question. Why don't they use their power to stop it? Just once and for all to stop it?*

*We cannot allow those children to die every day from starvation, from hunger, from violence, and their parents either dead like them or looking on. It's our fault.*

*ZAHN: You said you believe there are governments capable of stopping this. Why haven't they?*

*WIESEL: I don't know. Maybe they are busy with other tragedies. There are so many tragedies in the world, but everyone should be a priority.*

*But, on the other hand -- on one hand, you must say that I think this week, we have Secretary General Kofi Annan and Secretary of State Colin Powell, they are in Sudan, which is good.*

*For the first time, we have two men of such position, of such prestige, and they will see the tragedy with their own eyes. And they do have power. They can do something. They can at least alert the world.*

*ZAHN: So are you saying that the United Nations should play a lead role in this process with the United States?*

*WIESEL: If the two entities work together, they are unstoppable. Nobody can resist both the United Nations and the United States.*

On the same day Wednesday June 30, 2004, CNN.com reported:

"The United States circulated a resolution to member nations of the U.N. Security Council calling for sanctions against the militias being blamed for what has been described as a "humanitarian catastrophe" in Sudan. The resolution would place an arms embargo and travel restrictions on the so-called "Janjaweed" militias blamed for the abuses that have affected more than 2 million people in the western region of Darfur. U.N. Secretary-General Kofi Annan and U.S. Secretary of State Colin Powell are currently in Sudan, in an effort to pressure the Sudanese government to do more to build security and bring peace to the region."

Surely, anyone from southern Sudan will not be happy with this resolution. The resolution appears to be misplaced. Do you think sanctions against Militias will work? Who are the militias? And which countries trade with militias? The United States and the United Nations are missing the point here. Arab militias in Sudan are a creation of and are backed by the Sudanese government. If the US and the UN are serious about stopping the "civil war" in Sudan then, and at the very least, they should declare sanctions against the Sudanese government. And so far no formal action is proposed against the government of Sudan, despite charges it is behind the militia attacks.

What does this all mean now? It means that despite Collin Powell and Kofi Annan simultaneous visit to the Sudan, the world may not see much improvement to the people of southern Sudan because the powers that be have missed the point. Yes they will create awareness, but likely it will result in too much talk, little or nor action and hence no improvement at all.

Given the opportunity to suggest a solution, I would strongly propose either of two solutions. The first one is establishing a UN protected green zone free of Arab militias or the Janjaweeds. If Arab militias are found in this green zone they must be punished accordingly. Implementing this proposal would protect blacks in southern Sudan just as the "no fly zone" protected the Kurdis in Iraq under Sadam Husein's dictatorship.

The second solution would be dividing Sudan into two nations namely, North and South Sudan. I have seen a few of Sudanese brothers use South Sudan for country. I trust they believe this proposed solution would work just as North and South Korea worked. This proposal is important because it would eliminate the current problem of the north not accepting black leadership from the south of Sudan. It appears as if Arabs in northern Sudan believe black Sudanese in southern Sudan aught to be slaves. The world is different today, and the Sudanese government must come to terms with what is acceptable in the world today. Slavery is not acceptable. Black Africans make up 52 percent of Sudan's population, while Arabs make up 39 percent, according to the CIA. If the ground were level, and using a democratic model, the black majority would form government in Sudan.

As for the US and the UN much remains to be accomplished in Sudan apart from cheap talk. This is one case the rest of the world would be pleased to see the US, and perhaps Canada, take the lead at the UN and act to help the people in southern Sudan. TwCN.

# Time with Darci Lang

Once in a year, and at least in Canada, there is a week designated as public service week. The time is the second week of June. This week is set aside by an act of parliament to recognize the importance of public service employees and to create awareness of the critical services public service employees provide. Thank goodness!

Everyone's life is somewhat touched by the work of public servants. In Canada, public servants include municipal, provincial and federal government employees. These employees are motivated by very little other than their willingness to contribute in a positive way that makes a real difference in the lives of people. Anywhere you look around, you will see touch of public service employees. Whether you are thinking about the walkway in front of your home, or the lights on your street, or the running water that so many take for granted, or the driver's license in your wallet, or your provincial health card, your passport, your social insurance number card, or the traffic lights on the highway you drive to work – these all are provided by ordinary public servants, making real difference in your life. Yet, only few recognize that fact and take time to appreciate public servants.

Personally, I can't help it but to be proud of the fact that I am a public servant, and I am proud of my work. I realize that not everyone of the public appreciates the work provided by public servants, but I am always pleased to see that my work makes a real difference in the lives of people. And what do I do? Good question, but that is another subject all together. For now it must suffice to say I write and, I mine and crunch numbers.

In many countries it can be dreadful to be a public servant. I say so because by and large most people have no respect for public (civil) servants, who are most likely the least compensated for their work. But being a public servant in Canada makes me proud. First, because I am aware of the fact that the majority of people respect public servants. Secondly, I can afford to live on my salary, which is one thing I couldn't do when I was a public servant back in Zambia. Thirdly, there are many people out there who appreciate my work as a public servant. And to all who do, may I say thank you for your appreciation.

To celebrate the public service week (June 2004), I had the opportunity to attend a presentation by Darci Lang, President and CEO of Saskatchewan based X-L Enterprises, Inc., (www.darcilang.com). The woman's presentation was entitled, "Magnify Your Attitude: Focusing on the Positive 90%." In a nutshell the talk was about her own life.

Darci talked about how she was born to teenage parents, how she was raised by her father, who apparently married several times, she talked about her experience in tuxedo rental business and how she has no college or university education. Being one who appreciates higher education, I was somehow taken aback when Darci reminded me and others that she had no credentials to add to her name. Yet she has made it big in her profession as a professional speaker and trainer. "How true could this be in Canada?" I pondered. "What is her secret?"

Her sweet voice and her beauty, are perhaps her business's only assets. But the real secret to her success is positive thinking and hard work. And most importantly, her secret to success is simply focusing on and magnifying the 90 percent positive things in her life rather than on the 10 percent negative things. The woman has a career, a family, friends, a supportive husband, a place to live – and so she is happy. She has taken time to count her blessings and she has chosen to be happy given the positive things she already has.

I learnt a lot from Darci. So I learnt that whether it be my job, or my co-workers, or my friends, or my family, or even myself, to be happy I have to focus on and magnify the 90 percent positive things. I learnt never to allow the 10 percent negative things in my life determine my happiness and the extent there of it.

What is the overall lesson here? The overall lesson here is ATTITUDE. Yes, your attitude will determine how you face up to challenges. You can choose to be optimistic or pessimistic. If you choose to be an optimist you will magnify the 90 percent positive things in your life, energize yourself and forge forward as an achiever. But I hesitate to say, don't be pessimistic. Pessimists look for someone to blame for their misdeeds or misfortunes. Don't blame anyone. Rather do as Darci recommends, "Magnify your attitude: focusing on the positive 90 percent."

Now, if you like what you have read, don't thank me. Thank Darci. And if you just happen to be one who is not so easily pleased, let me know what you would like an ordinary public servant like me do to please you. TwCN.

# The World's Worst Evils

I t is said that laughter is the world's common language. And I needed a laugh, but it somehow eluded me. I started thinking about some really serious stuff, when in the process I recalled Nelson Mandela's line saying, "I hated them, because they looked good outside, but they were evil inside." At this point, I thought of conducting research on the world's worst evils. More so, because today it is getting more and more difficult to distinguish between what is evil and what is not evil. Society appears to be so indifferent to the appearance of evil.

From the top of my head, and considering the motives and the effects, I thought the world's worst evils would include colonialism, slavery, apartheid, genocide, terrorism, communism, and the like. But when I listened to one of the world's powerful leaders President Bush of the United States, it appears an evil like genocide is less evil than terrorism. So people can kill each other in Africa and perhaps Asia, and the world would still be called safer. As long as it does not happen in America, the world is safer. "How can it be?" I thought.

But another thought quickly came to mind, that perhaps I was too narrowly focused in my understanding. "Why shouldn't I research the internet and see, may be, I could find better material to qualify for world's worst evils?" I again thought. Yes, I found some really interesting evils. See if you can make anything out of each one of them.

### Breaking the mirror

*"I am so sick of myself!, all of me. There are three people who we play in this life. There is the first, who we show to others around us. There is the second,*

130

*which people perceive us as. Then there is the third, which is the inevitable truth of who we are inside and cannot hide from ourselves at the end of the day. I look in the mirror and I see a lost face. My features look like they were just randomly thrown together. That doesn't matter, I know I am attractive, I already have had that validated. But I am sick of second guessing myself, sick of over analyzing the situation when I get scared. I am SICK OF BEING SCARED. Not everyone is going to hurt me, not everyone is out to hurt me. I can converse sure, I can smile and make people laugh...why do I have to be so scared of what will happen if I let someone in? I don't want to hurt anymore and I certainly don't want to make someone else hurt. Maybe I was getting at something when the barista handed me that hand full of quarters and nickles and I said "No, No - I hate change."* - Anonymous.

Don't be bothered by your looks. God took care to create you. Be happy. And do as God wants you to do – first love him and appreciate how he created you, then love your neighbor as yourself.

### Parking too close!

*"You know what gets me angry? When people parallel park and for some unknown reason, decide to park bumper to bumper with your front/rear bumper! It's as if they don't care if you catch them doing it so blatantly."* - Anonymous

### My abusive mom

*"I really hate when my mom calls me just to tell me cheerfully that my stepsister lost her job. Does she think by telling me this I'm going to be happy? That this is going to cheer me up or something? I can hear the excitement in her voice. The thing is I've been dealing with this for years. One time I did tell her I don't like hearing her putting down my stepsister, she's such a nice girl. She tolerated my mom for years. Is there anyone out there who has experience like this? Man! I'm really frustrated, I want to stand up to her. She might pretend she has a nervous breakdown or something."* - Anonymous.

If the world did not have abusive moms, let alone dads, perhaps everyone would learn to love and do no evil. And we would all live in harmony and fully enjoy life.

### I bought some great jeans!

*"Want all the charm and personality that comes with old faded clothing, but don't want to wait years for your clothes to become worn out? Don't worry because now you can buy all the personality and attitude you want by owning your own pair of poorly made pre-packaged faded jeans. Now all your friends will think you're cool and original because wearing faded jeans is the hip thing to do. Never mind the piles and piles of used faded clothing you can buy at thrift stores for 1/50'th of the cost of new faded jeans. Your objective is to look cool and there's no better way than to buy new clothes that come worn out because it means that you can afford to spend your money on expensive jeans while people who wear naturally faded clothing usually do so because they can't afford new clothes.*

*Here's an idea: if you want to wear faded clothes so that you look like you can't afford new clothes, then why don't you buy real faded clothes from a thrift shop and give away the rest of your money to someone who will spend it on buying NEW clothes that they need most?* - Anonymous

What a thought! Sure somewhere in Africa, Southeast Asia, South America and inner cities of the West, someone would make good use of all the money spent buying faded jeans. But someone with an entrepreneurial spirit thought that money spent on new clothes must as well be spent to buy fashion.

### Parking Tickets

*"I always get parking tickets at UMCP. No matter where or what time I park, I always go back to my car and find a 20 dollar parking ticket. The parking people must lurk in the bushes or something."* – Anonymous.

It appears to me that the world needs people who ought to be confident about themselves, and believe in themselves. The world needs loving mothers and fathers, and supportive families. It seems the world needs people who can share what they have with those who have less or nothing. The world needs not only considerate drivers, but also responsible drivers.

But is there such a thing as the world's worst evil? Don't miss the point. There is no such thing as the world's worst evil. Evil is evil.

And there is no barometer to measure evil. But when it is inflicted, the victim knows it.

Also, what may appear to be worse to you, may not be necessarily worse to someone else. And therein lies the challenge. In today's world, though many people dream to rid the world of evil, the challenge is to identify evil in this somewhat indifferent world. But I hope when you see it, you will know it and work to stop it.

Should everyone hope to find solutions to all their evil or problems from someone else? May be not. Rather individuals as well as communities need to realize that they are likely the best and the best positioned to find solutions to their evil or problems. And this is not to say little help is not welcome and need not be rendered. TwCN.

# When Balance Is An Imperative

B alance is a commonly used word. And wherever it is used it shows there is concern. Balance is important in many aspects of life. For instance, I first head of the word balance being used seriously while a kid listening to my teacher talking about a balanced diet. Do you remember?

According to ADAM Inc., a balanced diet is "intake of appropriate types and adequate amounts of foods and drinks to supply nutrition and energy for maintenance of body cells, tissues, and organs, and to support normal growth and development," (www.adam.com). The term "balanced" simply means that a diet adequately meets your nutritional needs while not providing any nutrients in excess. A well-balanced diet acts to provide sources of energy and nutrition for optimal growth and development.

To achieve a balanced diet one must eat a variety of foods from all the food groups, including proteins, carbohydrates, minerals and vitamins. Sources of protein include milk and milk products such as cheese and yogurt; meat and meat substitutes such as chicken, fish, beef; legumes such as beans and peas and nuts and seeds. Sources of vitamins and minerals include fruits and vegetables. Sources of carbohydrates include grain and grain products such as whole grain breads, enriched breads and pastor, potatoes and cereals.

The most important step to eating a balanced diet is to educate yourself with what your body needs, and read the nutrition label and ingredients of all the food that you eat. Also, conditions such as diabetes, cholesterol problems, problems associated with your heart will determine the kind of balanced diet you take. It doesn't hurt to discuss your diet with your family physician or your personal dietician, that is if you can afford one.

Balance is not only important with diet, but also in business. The term "balanced scorecard" is commonly used in business. The balanced scorecard is a relatively new approach to strategic management of business pioneered by Drs. Robert Kaplan of Harvard Business School and David Norton. The balanced scorecard approach to managing business provides a clear prescription as to what companies and/or organizations, including government should measure in order to 'balance' and provide understanding of the financial perspective.

In years past and previous to the 1990s, in order to measure performance, businesses focused on financial data. But financial data was just one score on business performance. There was need to have scores on other aspects of business as well. These aspects include staff, customers, technology and business processes. So Kaplan and Norton introduced a scorecard that would achieve balanced planning and reporting on all important aspects of business. Therefore, the balanced scorecard suggests that an organization must be viewed from four perspectives, namely the learning and growth perspective (or employee development), the business process perspective (or technology), the customer perspective, and the financial perspective (or traditional approach).

Using a balanced scorecard, today's leaders of businesses and/or organizations are not only able to appreciate financial data that demonstrates excellent performance, but are also able to know from where and how the data is being generated.

Balance is not only important with diet and business, but it is also important in politics and government. This week, those of us in Canada, saw Prime Minister Paul Martin exercise his privilege and take the opportunity to constitute a Cabinet for the Canadian government following the June 28 election. His strategy for success has been to have a balanced cabinet. In such a geographically vast country and socially diverse nation as Canada, knowing what to balance and achieving acceptable balance can be a challenge, a daunting task. Balance need be achieved with respect to region, gender, ethnicity and language to name just some of the concerns.

But for wise and for leaders who are committed to building their countries, achieving balance within acceptable limits is no problem. Politics aside, Paul Martin demonstrated his wise leadership and tried to achieve balance in his cabinet. It is a cabinet of thirty-eight and inclusive of the west (8), the north (1), the east (4), women (8), and minorities (1). As expected and understandably, Ontario and Quebec lead in representation. Only the unreasonably critical would not be satisfied with such a cabinet. True to the saying: you cannot satisfy everyone. Like with every other balance imperative, all Canadians have to wait to see what this inclusive cabinet will deliver.

Being an African-Canadian, a touch on politics always reminds me of African politics. Challenges experienced in Canada vis-à-vis regionalism, language, gender, to name but just a few, are not unique to Canada. They are common world over, but of much interest is Africa. At the root of problems experienced in a good number of African countries (Sudan, Zimbabwe, Rwanda, DRC, to name just a few) are, one would suppose, due to uneven representation or sharing of power. I wish all African leaders can be reasonable, sensitive and responsive to the need for achieving balance in their governments. Being transparent and providing reasons for any appointments to cabinet and other significant government positions would go a long way in satisfying many a people and aspiring leaders in Africa. But would anyone get the message?

Not only is balance important in diet, business, politics and government, but also between work and family, and study and leisure. In this fast paced world, and particularly in the western hemisphere, it is increasingly difficult to find balance between work and family. Yet, it is important. How is your balance between work and family, or study and leisure?

Nowadays, it is not uncommon to see professionals 'marry' themselves to work, and students 'marry' themselves to studies. In as much as the results are admirable, there is a down side. Results include aging without family, or graduating without social skills, both of which are critical for personal development and well-being. Lack of balance between work and family, and study and leisure also shows fundamentally that someone lacks organizational and planning skills.

Finding balance between work and family, or study and leisure calls for daily planning accounting for each and every minute, and being well organized. If you realize that you have not achieved balance in your diet, balance between work and family, or study and leisure, you will do well to consider change and discipline yourself to get organized and develop a plan that will help you achieve the balance you need so much in your life.

Finally, and at this point, it must be appropriate to say looking for balance is a good dream. The challenge, of course, is how to achieve it. And it is good to know that you can if you put your mind to it and treat it as an imperative. Balance in your diet, balance in your business, balance between your work and family, or your studies and leisure, is a wonderful desire and it is achievable. Should you have opportunity to influence politics, demand balance in representation considering region, gender, ethnicity, language and whatever is important. All in all, it must be indisputable that balance is indeed an imperative. TwCN

# Why So Many of Us Relate to Barack Obama

He is, as Bose Agbayewa (President of the Nigerian Association of Manitoba) would describe him, "eloquent, impeccably knowledgeable of the issues and above all, comfortable and proud of who he is." A forty-two year old African-American, son of a black African man from Kenya and a white American woman from Kansas. "I am sure that many of us were shedding tears of joy for seeing somebody who represented us so well. Africa should be very proud!" wrote Agbayewa about Barack Obama in her e-mail to the African community in Manitoba.

There are many reasons why so many in Africa and America would relate to Barack Obama. And Obama brought out many of these reasons in his speech to the Democratic National Convention on Tuesday, July 27, 2004.

*1. Larger Dreams*

Obama reflected on the dreams of his father early in his speech. Listen to what he had to say: *"My father was a foreign student, born and raised in a small village in Kenya. He grew up herding goats, went to school in a tin-roof shack. His father, my grandfather, was a cook, a domestic servant. But my grandfather had larger dreams for his son. Through hard work and perseverance my father got a scholarship to study in a magical place; America which stood as a beacon of freedom and opportunity to so many who had come before."*

This sounds so familiar. Many of us who have come out of Africa to live in the Diaspora can relate to what Obama summarizes here.

The majority of African intellectuals were raised in small villages or towns. They grew up herding some animals or cultivating on peasant farms, walked some good number of kilometers to school, and the school was likely a "tin-roof shack". I know some Africans don't like to be so blatant about anything that conveys negative connotations. And that is understandable and appreciated. But we all must be proud of our back grounds as Obama is of his, if we have to position ourselves for bringing about real change. Most of the parents invested the little that they had in their first or second child who went to school. Through hard work and perseverance these rural boys and girls made it to secondary school, later to university, and thereafter secured scholarships to study in magical places commonly America, Canada and the UK.

Talking about his grandparents on the mother's side, Obama said: *"And they, too, had big dreams for their daughter, a common dream, born of two continents. My parents shared not only an improbable love; they shared an abiding faith in the possibilities of this nation. They would give me an African name, Barack, or "blessed," believing that in a tolerant America your name is no barrier to success. They imagined me going to the best schools in the land, even though they weren't rich, because in a generous America you don't have to be rich to achieve your potential."*

Many Africans who decide to live outside Africa, in order to achieve their dreams as well as the dreams for their children must not only share the improbable love but also the abiding faith in the opportunities and possibilities that the West has to offer. Being aware of the opportunities and possibilities that the West has to offer is key to finding ways to pursue and achieve one's larger dreams.

Obama talks about how he was given an African name, a name that had a meaning, believing that no name must be a barrier to success. This is revealing. And it is good to see that many Africans today are giving their children African names. One reason being that names must have a meaning and in Africa most names do. The second reason being that your name must be no barrier to success, not only in America and Canada, but also everywhere in the world. Moreover, learning other people's names and being interested in using other people's names is a demonstration of respect and acceptance.

## 2. The Pride Of America

Obama also touched on the fundamental principle that makes America proud, and the envy of the world. Obama said, *"Tonight, we gather to affirm the greatness of our nation, not because of the height of our skyscrapers, or the power of our military, or the size of our economy. Our pride is based on a very simple premise, summed up in a declaration made over two hundred years ago,* **"We hold these truths to be self-evident, that all men are created equal. That they are endowed by their Creator with certain inalienable rights. That among these are life, liberty and the pursuit of happiness."**

When I heard these words I could not help but think of my motherland, Africa and Zambia in particular. I thought of the suffering people in Southern Sudan, I thought of troubled spots in Africa. I asked, "Why can't African leaders buy such a wonderful principle from the Americans?" I thought, Americans may not give you butter and bread for free, but one thing I am sure, they will give you this premise for free - respect for life, liberty and the right to pursue happiness. What more can Africans ask for of their leaders and the world?

Obama added, *"That is the true genius of America, a faith in the simple dreams of its people, the insistence on small miracles. That we can tuck in our children at night and know they are fed and clothed and safe from harm. That we can say what we think, write what we think, without hearing a sudden knock on the door. That we can have an idea and start our own business without paying a bribe or hiring somebody's son. That we can participate in the political process without fear of retribution, and that our votes will be counted-or at least, most of the time."*

Here Obama reminded me that the needs of the Americans are no different from the needs of the Africans – civil liberties, security, entrepreneurship, and democracy. But while America builds and grows, evidence shows Africa demolishes and destroys. Surely, how wonderful it would be for African leaders to reconsider their positions, and come to their senses. And rather than waste people's lives, work to help their people and build their countries and make Africa proud. Yes, the pride of America can be the pride of Africa, as well as the pride of the world.

*3. Connected As One People*

Obama scored many points in his speech. Considering the pursuant of the American dream in the context of diversity of America, Obama said, *"For alongside our famous individualism, there's another ingredient in the American saga. A belief that we are connected as one people. If there's a child on the south side of Chicago who can't read, that matters to me, even if it's not my child. If there's a senior citizen somewhere who can't pay for her prescription and has to choose between medicine and the rent, that makes my life poorer, even if it's not my grandmother. If there's an Arab American family being rounded up without benefit of an attorney or due process, that threatens my civil liberties. It's that fundamental belief-I am my brother's keeper, I am my sisters' keeper-that makes this country work. It's what allows us to pursue our individual dreams, yet still come together as a single American family. "E pluribus unum." Out of many, one."*

Having come from Africa and living in North America, I have had the benefit of experiencing four worlds – African, Zambian, Canadian and North American. So I understand what Obama is saying. Many of us in the Diaspora see the value of being connected as one people. And true is Obama's words! There are some of those leaders in Africa who make a mistake thinking that those in the Diaspora are not part of them. Yet deep in our hearts, those of us in the Diaspora, know we are part of those at home. And even as a community of Africans in the Diaspora we know we are all connected, and more importantly connected regardless of our economic or social status.

Obama went on to say, *"There's not a black America and white America and Latino America and Asian America; there's the United States of America. The pundits like to slice-and-dice our country into Red States and Blue States; Red States for Republicans, Blue States for Democrats. But I've got news for them, too. We worship an awesome God in the Blue States, and we don't like federal agents poking around our libraries in the Red States."*

Yes, our approach to life must transcend race, language and regionalism, so that regardless of race, language and regionalism we are all connected. Most importantly, Africa is made up of many types of people, including blacks, whites, Arabs, Asians, etc. But there is no better way to look at Africa than the way Obama put it for America. There must not be a black African, white African, Arab

African and Asian African or French and English African; there must only be one Africa. What a dream! But as everyone knows the pundits like to slice-and-dice the continent into Arab, black, white or French and English or tribes, etc. And unfortunately thousands and millions of precious lives are lost in the process. At this moment, my heart goes to the people of Sudan.

*4. Hope Is On The Way*

Being aware that desperation kills, Obama was quick to point out and remind the citizens of the world that we all need hope to survive. Believing in the vision of his party's leadership Obama said: *"John Kerry calls on us to hope. John Edwards calls on us to hope. I'm not talking about blind optimism here-the almost willful ignorance that thinks unemployment will go away if we just don't talk about it, or the health care crisis will solve itself if we just ignore it. No, I'm talking about something more substantial. It's the hope of slaves sitting around a fire singing freedom songs; the hope of immigrants setting out for distant shores; . . . the hope of a millworker's son who dares to defy the odds; the hope of a skinny kid with a funny name who believes that America has a place for him, too. The audacity of hope!"*

If you are an immigrant like me you know what Obama is talking about. If you are an African from a developing country like Zambia, where there is so much unemployment, and the health care system is in tatters, you know what Obama is talking about. If you live in the West, and you have a 'funny' African name, you know what Obama is talking about. If you are a new immigrant in Canada and your credentials cannot be recognized, and so you do some odd jobs while going to school, you know what Obama is talking about. But you can have hope than one day, with perseverance and hard work, the sun will rise on you. Even those in Africa where leaders seem to plunder the only resources that can be used to create employment and improve health care, must have hope that one day the sun will rise even in form of sane leaders whose only interest will be to better the lives of people. It is hope that must carry you and me through the process of achieving our dreams.

Just in case there are critics against the possibility of achieving dreams, hear how Obama puts it, *"In the end, that is God's greatest gift to us, the bedrock of this nation; the belief in things not seen; the belief that there are better days ahead."* How true it is that better days always come after hardship days. For there is no freedom unless there is slavery. There is no life unless there is some birth pain. There is no arrival unless there is travel. Yes, it is true. Whether it is in your life or my life, "Hope is on the way."

*5. What You Need To Achieve Your Dream*

Obama surely seems to have it all. He does not only dream, but he knows how to face up the challenges and move towards fulfilling his dream. To this end, Obama said, *"Tonight, if you feel the same energy I do, the same urgency I do, the same passion I do, the same hopefulness I do-if we do what we must do, then I have no doubt that . . . . this country will reclaim its promise, and out of this long political darkness a brighter day will come. Thank you and God bless you."*

For you and me to achieve our dreams, to reclaim the promises of opportunities and possibilities, wherever we may be on the globe, we need energy, we need urgency, we need passion, we need to be hopeful, and we need to do what we must do. Finally, as all great American speakers end, we need to ask for God's blessing of everything we do, and thank him for all his blessings. TwCN.

# Dual Citizenship: A Win-Win Strategy - Part 1

I f you asked my mom whether she knows me as a talkative or quiet person, I trust she would tell you that I am a quiet person. No arguments, she knows me better for I am her son.

But often, it is the short and impromptu conversations with friends like you that get my mind going. And this week I had a ten minute conversation with a Ugandan-Canadian friend. He related how at last Uganda is considering the possibility of recognizing dual citizenship for its citizens. Then I thought of Ghana, Nigeria, Canada, the US and a host of other countries. But before I make you overly interested in dual citizenship, I wish to share a true Zambian story, first told by Felix Kunda in 1998.

*Zambia, A Question of Citizenship*
*By Felix Kunda*

"Mr. Majid Ticklay (59) is an alien among his own children, being the only person in his own family who is not Zambian. His three sons and one daughter are Zambians by birth, likewise his brother. So, how come Majid Ticklay is in such a predicament?

Mr. Ticklay's story started with his father, the late Mohammed Hussein Ticklay, who emigrated from India in 1938 to set up business in Zambia, then called Northern Rhodesia. He stayed long enough in Zambia to establish himself and then returned to India to get his family. This was in 1946. The young Majid Ticklay accompanied his father back to Zambia at the age of eight. Since then he has lived in Zambia.

His father had opened two retail shops in Monze and Kaleya (in Zambia's southern province). These shops were especially helpful to the local African population, at a time when non-whites were not allowed to buy from certain shops because of existing apartheid practices. For his services, Mohammed Ticklay was appointed the first non-white town councillor in Mazabuka. He served on the council for ten years.

**Citizenship problems** - Zambia became independent on 24 October 1964. The Constitution stated that all British living in the new country were to be considered citizens of that country, unless they chose not to be. Indians, too, were included in this specification. But then the government decreed that Indians had to apply for citizenship, and in 1968, their applications to become Zambians were turned down.

About the same time, Zambia was going through a period of economic reforms and a decree was enacted prohibiting non- Zambians from owning and operating retail shops. Shop-owners who were thus affected, became destitute overnight.

But the Ticklay family did not sit idle and mourn over spilled milk. Instead, two years on, they established other retail businesses and registered them in the name of Majid Ticklay's brother who was born in the country after independence, and therefore a Zambian by birth.

By 1985, Majid Ticklay assumed his father's mantle as head of the family business in Zambia. But tragedy was to strike. Armed robbers attacked his house in Lusaka during the night and killed four family members. Although seriously injured, his wife survived the attack and lived on for a further two years.

**Public service** - Obviously, Ticklay was deeply affected by these events, and so when he was approached by the Makeni Neighbourhood Watch to join them, he didn't need much persuading. He gave all his spare time supporting this organisation, even using his own car for patrolling the area against robbers. Eventually he was asked to become chairman of his local Neighbourhood Watch, and he accepted this as a challenge to assist the residents of Makeni in fighting crime and as a means of serving his local community.

Ticklay's participation in public life has increased. He is a committee member of the Lusaka Chamber of Commerce, a member of the Lusaka Rotary Club and is active in community work.

With this background, it's little wonder that the people of Chawama constituency chose Ticklay as their candidate for parliament, not knowing that in spite of all his activities in social work and living in the country for 51 years, he still was not a Zambian.

**Applying for citizenship** - In November 1994, Majid Ticklay reapplied (the second time) for Zambian citizenship, hoping that his application would be received favourably in time to stand for election in the 1996 elections. Nothing happened, and in April 1997 he was notified by the Home Affairs Minister that his request for citizenship had been refused.

But Mr. Ticklay remains undeterred. He says that Zambia is "home". His father died at the age of 80, and is buried in Mazabuka. Mr Majid Ticklay is determined that he, too, will die in his country of adoption. He loves Zambia and its people and this gives him strength to assist the underprivileged. He feels that the Zambian government, in denying him Zambian citizenship, is denying him his basic human rights.

Mr Ticklay currently holds a British Overseas Passport and therefore, he is neither British, Indian or Zambian. To all intents and purposes, he is stateless.

His legal situation is as follows: According to Zambia's Constitution, anyone domiciled in Zambia for ten years, can apply for Zambian citizenship. Mr. Ticklay has applied, his application has been refused, but the government has failed to provide him with reasons for this refusal.

Or is there a political motive? Could it be that Majid Ticklay is considered by the ruling Movement for Multi-Party Democracy (MMD) government to be a threat to sitting Chawama Member of Parliament, General Christon Tembo, who is Zambia's Vice-President?

Despite being extremely popular in Zambia, Majid Ticklay remains an alien among his own people." END. (*Reproduced with express permission from ANB-BIA SUPPLEMENT, Issue/Edition No. 341 - 01/03/1998.*)

*Where Do We Go From Here*

Why should TwCN make you read an article about a case of citizenship in Zambia, Africa and not the US or Canada? First, here are a few questions to ponder. Why should one wait for 10 years before he/she can become a citizen? Why should a law abiding alien be denied citizenship? Why should someone willing to invest, create employment, and serve the community be denied citizenship? There is something, and I don't want to call it wrong, but there is something to seriously consider for improvement.

Secondly, Mr. Majid Ticklay's dream was to become a Zambian citizen, and remain motivated to contribute to the development of Zambia. But he was turned down. As in every battle there are losers and winners, surely there was a loser in this battle too.

Kunda's article sets a stage for looking at the merits and demerits of dual citizenship. And the next edition of TwCN compares and contrasts the case of citizenship in the first and third worlds, and shows how dual citizenship has been a win-win strategy for the first world. Hopefully, we will see how Zambia, and the rest of the developing world, could benefit from recognizing dual citizenship. TwCN.

# Dual Citizenship: A Win-Win Strategy - Part 2

You possess dual or multiple citizenship when more than one country recognizes you as its citizen. Kunda's article provided in TwCN (33) set a stage for looking at the merits and demerits of dual citizenship. And TwCN (34) compares and contrasts the case of citizenship in the first and third worlds, and arguably shows how dual citizenship has been a win-win strategy for the first or developed world.

*DC-The Developed Country Initiative for Prosperity*

A good number of industrialized countries of the West have one thing in common – recognition of dual citizenship. These countries include Switzerland, Canada, United Kingdom, and the United States of America. Other countries of interest that recognize dual citizenship in special cases include Nigeria, South Africa and Israel.

One fact that hit me is that most of the countries that recognize dual citizenship also enjoy a great degree of prosperity. Consider Switzerland, for example. About Switzerland the CIA World Fact Book says: "*Switzerland is a prosperous and stable modern market economy with low unemployment, a highly skilled labor force, and a per capita GDP larger than that of the big Western European economies. The Swiss in recent years have brought their economic practices largely into conformity with the EU's to enhance their international competitiveness. Switzerland remains a safe haven for investors, because it has maintained a degree of bank secrecy and has kept up the franc's long-term external value.*" With a Gross Domestic Product (GDP) per capita of $32,000, Switzerland has no known population that lives below the poverty line.

Before coming to the West I saw people who were very excited at the opportunity to go to the East – Soviet Union, East German, Hungary, etc. If you lived during those days you must be chuckling now. But I came to the West, and to be frank, without any real strategy for my future. Luckily, I came to Canada where, for hardworking people, it's never too late to catch up.

About Canada as a developed country the CIA World Fact Book says: *"As an affluent, high-tech industrial society, Canada today closely resembles the US in its market-oriented economic system, pattern of production, and high living standards. Since World War II, the impressive growth of the manufacturing, mining, and service sectors has transformed the nation from a largely rural economy into one primarily industrial and urban. . . . . Nevertheless, given its great natural resources, skilled labor force, and modern capital plant Canada enjoys solid economic prospects. . . . Another long-term concern is the flow south to the US of professionals lured by higher pay, lower taxes, and the immense high-tech infrastructure. A key strength in the economy is the substantial trade surplus."*

Relative to dual citizenship, when these developed countries drafted their constitutions, they realized that they needed to create environments that would allow for both direct and indirect flow of both financial and intellectual capital in and out of the country. Some, like the British deliberately scattered their subjects around the globe, and ensured that as the colonies attained their independence the subjects still remained British citizens. But individual subjects also reserved their liberty and rights to denounce British citizenship if they so wished.

*DC-Advantage or Disadvantage*

Yes, the economic reason is the most compelling reason why developed countries have chosen to recognize dual citizenship. Dual citizenship offers practical advantages, e.g. social security or employment. It may also enhance individual's feeling of belonging, because they have strong personal ties to more than one country. Citizens who have these advantages, naturally work harder in order to live comfortably in the country of residence and to benefit people in the native country.

But dual citizenship is not without disadvantages. Some countries have laws that do not apply to foreign visitors, but which apply to citizens — for example, restrictions on exit, compulsory military service, and special taxes or financial compensation for services received in the past. There might be special circumstances relating to only those with dual citizenship—for example, friends or relatives may be affected by visits by one with dual citizenship. Sometimes there may be complicated legalities.

Dual citizenship might be affected if countries of which one is a citizen are involved in political upheavals or military conflicts. In today's world, this is particularly more probable for citizens of Middle East countries, Israel and the United States than any other country.

Although dual citizenship may have disadvantages, the cases are different and some of these drawbacks may or may not be applicable. It is just important to be aware of them.

*DC Not Common in Developing Countries*

Most developing countries do not recognize dual or multiple citizenship. This is amazing as well as fascinating. Without taking away from the rights of sovereign countries to enact citizenship laws, it is just amazing to see that in today's world, where most developing countries depend on economic and financial aid from developed countries, and citizens of developing countries continue to leave there native countries to pursue dreams in developed countries, governments cannot consider dual citizenship as an indirect way of allowing for capital flow from developed countries. Surely, most immigrants in developed countries have strong ties with their native countries. And they would like their children, when ever possible, to maintain these ties. But, and unfortunately, most immigrants to the West cannot have dual citizenship as it is not recognized by their native developing countries.

It is in this light that it is encouraging to see that Uganda is entertaining the idea of recognizing dual citizenship. And any country with a good number of its nationals outside its boundaries would surely benefit from dual citizenship. This would be true for

African countries like Sierra Leone, Zambia, Zimbabwe, Kenya, and DRC to name but few.

Furthermore, Kunda's Zambian story made a very interesting reading. But it left a number of questions to ponder. *"Why should one wait for 10 years before he/she can become a citizen? Why should a law abiding alien be denied citizenship? Why should someone willing to invest, create employment, and serve the community be denied citizenship?"*

Research by TwCN shows that citizenship laws are complicated. And because of their complication few countries take time to review them and improve upon them to address modern-day needs. So was the case in Zambia at the time Mr. Ticklay applied for Zambian citizenship. The 10 year waiting period was based on the British system of laws (commonly referred to as UKC-Commonwealth) which were adopted and adapted by the former British colonies, including Zambia. But countries such as Canada and Australia that have taken time to review their laws in light of their needs, which includes immigration, have actually changed this requirement. As those in Canada know, Canada requires one to be resident for only three years before they can apply for citizenship. Australia requires only two years of residence before granting citizenship.

The fact that every country has the right to confer citizenship on the people that it accepts is well appreciated. But to deny citizenship to a law abiding citizen without providing proper reasons appears to be injustice of one form or another. Particularly when a person has demonstrated his capability to constructively contribute to the development of the country, one would think that the government would be vying to see such a person become a citizen. Unfortunately, it wasn't the case for Mr. Ticklay in Zambia. No surprise to many especially that Zambia was once known to be a country with a government that attempted to strip citizenship from its former president of 30 years. Seriously speaking, there is room for improvement in the Zambian Citizenship Act.

*DC-Catalyst for Attaining Individual and*
*National Dreams*

In TwCN (33) it was written, *"Mr. Majid Ticklay's dream was to become a Zambian citizen, and remain motivated to contribute to the development of Zambia. But he was turned down. As in every battle there are losers and winners, surely there was a loser in this battle too."*

Recognizing dual or multiple citizenship calls for a government to see advantages beyond someone's skin color or accent or political motives. This calls for a government to understand how economic gains are appropriated and how skills, capabilities and talents are acquired relatively cheap through grant of citizenship. Yes, there may be drawbacks of dual or multiple citizenship, but they don't significantly compare with the gains or merits.

Consider the case of Greece's 2004 Olympics Baseball Team, for example. As a host country, Greece is entitled to fielding a team in every sport. Greece has no baseball league, but the country needed a baseball team. They had to make a special provision to acquire baseball talent for the Olympic team. Here is what TwCN research uncovered:

*"Ideally, the Greek National Team would be comprised of citizens of Greece; however, it is unlikely that Greek baseball players can reach a level of proficiency soon enough to play competitively in 2004.*

*Therefore, the Greek government, in cooperation with the International Olympic Committee, has agreed that any person of Greek descent who has at least one grandparent (from either side of the family) born in Greece qualifies to participate in the 2004 Olympics.*

*High school and college baseball players with ability, as well as professional players of Greek descent, who wish to take advantage of this unique opportunity to pursue their dreams of playing in the Olympic Games should contact the Baltimore Orioles."* (Source: www.baseballgreece.com/olympic.html).

Needless to say that the Greek Baseball Team has been constituted. But as you can see the situation would have been even better and easier if Greece recognized dual citizenship. Nevertheless, as some people would say 'thank goodness,' *"Greek law does not automatically remove citizenship upon a person acquiring a foreign citizenship. When a Greek citizen acquires another nationality, they are technically a dual citizen until the Greek government has given permission for the removal of Greek citizenship."* - Multiplecitizenship.com.

*DC-One Indirect Key to Prosperity*

The dream for most developing countries is to prosper as the industrialized countries of the West, particularly Canada, UK and the US. The challenge for developing countries, however, is to change the legal and economic system that serves as catalyst for economic prosperity. The dream of economic prosperity can partly be accomplished by improving upon the citizenship laws, and beginning to recognize dual citizenship.

Yes, dual citizenship can be a win-win strategy. It has been for the major developed countries of the West. For sure, it could be for developing countries too, particularly those from Africa. It may look trivial, but in today's economically competitive world, every bit of advantage counts. TwCN.

# No Scary Dreams for Ambitious Optimists

I could imagine the days when British colonizers dreamed of conquering the world. And by and large they did it. I could imagine the days when American founders dreamed of a free country, truly democratic and committed to protecting the rights of individuals. And by and large they achieved it. I could imagine the time when great American Scientists dreamed of walking on the moon and in space. And by and large they achieved it. I could imagine the days when the Wright Brothers dreamed of flying. And by and large they did it.

I could also imagine the days when non-dreamers and pessimists could call such dreams as 'too ambitious, they are scary'. But the dreamers believed in their dreams and in themselves. And so despite adversity, they pushed forward until they fulfilled their ambitions.

*Ambition of the Ambitious*

By the way, what is ambition? Roget's New Millennium Thesaurus (Lexico Publishing Group, LLC) defines ambition, in its function as a noun, as a drive, desire, goal, hope, thought, want, and dream, to give but a few of the meanings. Individuals who have ambitions are described as being ambitious, an adjective of ambition. To be ambitious means to be driven, effortful, hopeful, combative, challenging, hard, anxious, and resourceful, again to use but a few meanings.

Recently, I heard someone describe the Manitoba African Community leaders dream for the African-Canadian Cultural and Heritage

Centre, or simply put African Centre, which is well outlined in a Business Plan as "ambitious and scary." I like the description, because it qualifies the quest of the African Community in Manitoba to acquire the African Centre as a real dream. And like all real dreams are fulfilled, Africans in Manitoba can see a day when an African Centre will stand in Manitoba.

For pessimists the dream of an African Centre is an impossible dream. Yet it is possible, and very possible indeed to those of interest, those who are ambitious optimists. The African Centre will materialize in Manitoba if those who are optimists take it, as they have already done, as their goal, desire, drive, hope, thought and dream to have the African Centre. Yes, the African Centre may be challenging, but the optimists, those leaders who are ambitious must live to the meaning of the word - being goal driven, effortful, hopeful, combative and resourceful. Being mindful that there is strength in numbers and putting forth a united front is critical. Soon and very soon we will see the African Centre in Manitoba.

*Why the African Centre?*

If you are not from Manitoba, but you are like those intelligent kids, you are probably already asking the 'why' question. Why the African Centre?

To answer your question, Kaonga from Zambia would tell you that there is need for a place to anchor African-Canadian kids. In Africa the whole village raises a child. There is need for a facility like an African village in Manitoba. And the African Centre would serve as a village. A mother could leave her kids there knowing that the kids would be with the people she knows, just like in an African village.

Mutaka from the Democratic Republic of the Congo would tell you that if Africans had a home, they could put in place programs to help African kids, training them in math, science, and languages. Africans have come to Canada to stay. Africans are growing roots and need to be well planted. Africans desperately need a home, a place where kids would come and learn something not only about Africa, but also about Canada.

Kambamba from Sudan would tell you, Africans need a place for new arrivals in Manitoba. A place where new arrivals could feel welcome and get to know the people so they can be quickly integrated into the community. Also, African youths don't need to hang around Central Park. They need to have a place where they can go and meet with other youths, play together and socialize responsibly.

Amenyogbe from Ghana would tell you Africans in Manitoba left Africa to live in peace and prosperity in Canada. But they still miss their culture. They need a place where they can celebrate their culture and share it with the rest of Canadians.

Onyebuchi from Nigeria would tell you that the African Centre would make the people of Manitoba proud. People from around the world would come to the African Centre to discuss critical issues affecting the continent of Africa.

Every African you ask, will tell you a good reason why Manitoba needs an African Centre.

*We know the reasons, what then?*

Never let anyone talk you out of your dreams. Imagine that God's dreams and ambitions are what make the world go around; and as it goes around in causes day and night and creates yesterday, today and the hope for tomorrow. Similarly, the dream of the African community in Manitoba is what will continually make the community grow and continue to succeed and prosper. From the burdens of war, refugee camps, and oppression in Africa, Africans will continue working hard and moving forward until they have a permanent home in the heartland of Canada even Winnipeg, Manitoba.

Since the African Centre is important to all Africans and other Canadians in Manitoba, there is need to know how to talk about it to government officials, friends, neighbors and community leaders. It is important to stick to only one theme or subject. You can choose to speak about how important the African Centre is to parents, or the youths, or new immigrants or the Government of Manitoba. It is important to be mindful of the fact that the African community needs tremendous support of everyone, including all Canadians and the three levels of government, and to some extent even outside help if it can be found. Africans must speak with one voice on each and every issue. Being careful to distinguish between express personal opinion and community consensus is key to helping us achieve unity. Community consensus must come first in all communications with those outside the African community. This communication strategy will help us to acquire the impetus we need to move forward toward achieving the grand dream – the African Centre.

*What about the cost?*

Building an African Centre, like any other projects requires, most importantly, financial resources. And like the Olympic Athletes compete for gold, silver or bronze, African community leaders are competing for the best resources that they can find. But if they cannot get the gold, should they settle for silver? I would guess yes, it's better than the bronze. If they get neither gold nor silver, should they settle for the bronze? I would guess yes, it's better than nothing. After all, some of the African leaders come from bronze rich countries – Zambia and the Democratic Republic of the Congo. However, what they should not settle for is nothing.

All in all, the dreams to see kids celebrating African culture at the African Centre, see kids learning math, science, and languages at the African Centre, see kids playing a ball game at the African Centre, must be kept alive and pursued. Good dreams, great dreams are never too ambitious. And there is no dream that is too ambitious and scary. Ambitious dreams are worthy challenging. Ambitious dreams are worthy fulfilling. And the African Centre in Manitoba is one such dream. TwCN.

# Olympic Games! Where The Truly Powerful Shine?

Since there inception in 776 BC, the Olympics have been admirable games of emotions. And you don't need to be an athlete to relate to the Olympics. The least you need is just to watch one game and see one athlete win a gold medal. As the medals are given, you will hear the national anthem of the gold medal winner's country. It is then that tears of joy are shed. It is then that you see athletes' dreams fulfilled.

*Medals make instant celebrities*

Winning a gold medal is every athlete's dream. For with gold comes the joy of hearing your country's national anthem and the opportunity to uplift your country to the forefront of the whole world. Athletes who win gold become instant celebrities assured of handshakes with VIPs, assured of corporate sponsorships, and above all assured of the attention of the media. Medal winners make their countries and people proud. No wonder so many athletes give in to steroids just so they can have the opportunity to win gold.

*Canadians lag behind in medals*

It is two days before the end of the Athens 2004 Olympic Games. Canada has managed to win only seven medals, and it is a worrisome accomplishment compared to the United States' 82 and China's 54 medals won and accomplished so far. Like all other countries participating at the Olympics, the dream of Canada is to shine at the Olympics. For Canada this dream is even more vivid given that she is a developed country comparable only to the likes of the US,

Germany, France, the UK, and Australia, each of which has managed to win at least 25 medals. One may be tempted to say that, given everything else, the Olympic Games is where the truly powerful shine. But why should a country like Canada perform so poorly at the Olympics? The problems resulting in failure to shine at the Olympics may be more deep rooted than Canadians realize.

*Canada's fundamental athlete problems*

There are supposedly three fundamental problems at the root of Canada's poor showing at the 2004 Olympic Games. The first and most commonly cited problem is the lack of adequate funding for athletes. In sports, athletes must have the money in order for them to devote more time to training rather than finding ways to survive. Money can be sourced from many sources including government and private organizations. One effective way to help athletes is to have private corporations behind athletes. This can be achieved by having a well organized sports system including strong professional and armature sports leagues, as well as college leagues. Some may argue Canada has done well in terms of organizing sport. And this is where the second fundamental problem comes in.

Secondly, Canada does not seem to have a pool of talent deep and wide as the US's or China's. With 30 million people of whom only 13 percent are youths, it is very difficult to produce well talented and proven athletes capable of winning medals consistently. Some people may argue that it is not the amount of talent, but rather the quality that counts. Sounds like a plausible argument. But in sports, competition is the driver and determinant of quality. Without a large pool of athletes, you cannot have competitive sports comparable to the world class Olympics. But even with a pool of talent deep and wide as the US's or China's, Canada still faces another challenge.

Canada's weather is such that it is mainly extreme winters. And you cannot produce world class athletes when the only time you have them to practice is three to six months in a year. Athletes need ample time to be on the field, and part of that time must be free reign practicing time. Free reign practicing time is where athletes play on their own discovering all kinds of tricks of the games and building up their confidence. Without free reign sport, athletes are limited to the coach's ideas and direction. They do not have opportunity to be creative.

Chrispin Ntungo

*Can Canadians learn from the USA, China and others?*

What is it about the US and China that makes them produce the world's finest athletes. One indisputable fact is that China and the US are populous countries having one billion and 292 million people, respectively. With this level of population, there are good chances that China and the US have every type of athlete the rest of the world has to offer. The only task for these two countries to do is to put in place a process that helps to seek out the best athletes from amongst their populations. So the process of selecting athletes in China and the US is such that it is so intensely competitive that in many ways it's no different from the Olympic Games. So by the time China and the US select there Olympic teams, they have the very best of athletes the world has to offer. So at the Olympic Games the US and China don't only win the very best of medals, but they win most of the medals.

What is it that Canada can do to reverse the trend? First, if you have gone to school in Canada, you will notice that students are discouraged from competition in their studies. Kids are taught there are no winners and failures. Brilliant and dull students are put together, and are provided the same opportunities for success. This policy sounds better on paper, but the result is worrisome. How do you expect kids who are raised in a noncompetitive environment to perform better at a competitive environment such as the Olympic Games?

Secondly, Canada has a competitive advantage in immigration. And Canada can use her immigration policy to lure talent from China, Africa, the US and Cuba. In the past Canada's gold medal winners have all been immigrants: Ben Johnson (Seoul, 1988, though stripped of gold because of drugs), Donovan Bailey (Atlanta 1996) and Daniel Igali (Sydney 2000), were all recent immigrants.

If Canadians really wanted to be powerful and shine at the summer Olympics, they would adopt a long term strategy and seek the talent. This talent can be found either by raising athletically competitive kids, or pursuing and admitting athletically competitive immigrants. Only then would Canada be assured of more medals at the summer Olympics than she is achieving now. TwCN.

# We Can Do Better For Newcomers and the Community

T his past week has been tough for the Winnipeg community which lost a fourteen year Eritrean and African boy whose parents moved to Winnipeg as refugees in 2000. The boy suffered and died of gunshot wounds. The parents are mourning. The community is grieving. The culprits are no where to be found. The victim will be laid to rest. But it is important to realize that there is a problem here whose source is deep rooted. And it is just as important to identify, or at least, remind us of the problem and possibly seek a remedy.

The late boy came to Winnipeg as a son of refugee parents. The parents, like all immigrants, had dreams for the boy, as well as for themselves. But how come those dreams could not come to fruition?

*The two sides of Winnipeg*

Winnipeg is a beautiful city. Its brighter side includes being not too large and not so sophisticated. From anywhere in Winnipeg, you can drive at 60 km per hour and get to the city centre within 20 minutes. Winnipeg is the capital of Manitoba which is known for its lovely number plate tag "Friendly Manitoba." The city is multicultural with people from all over the world including Asians, Africans, Europeans and South Americans.

But Winnipeg, like every city, also has a dark side, unfortunately! It still has very poor people who live below the poverty line. These people are concentrated in the inner city part of Winnipeg, which is the area within 5 to 8 km northwest and north of downtown Winnipeg. This area is characterized by low cost housing which is affordable for low income families or people on government social support.

Worse still is the fact that this area is a haven for drug and alcohol addicts and abusers. It is also the area where prostitutes parade themselves. During the day almost anyone in this area shows the friendly Manitoba face. But at night the area is a den of misfits – drug pushers and prostitutes.

*First acquaintance to Canada*

Canada is known for its humanitarian values and work of taking in refugees and helping them recover and lead gainful lives. It is an expensive venture and unfortunately it is not done the best way it ought to be. Why would one assert so?

One would assert so because when refugees arrive in Winnipeg on government support, they are accommodated in the inner-city of Winnipeg. Their first introduction and first acquaintance to Canada is the inner-city. In the inner-city most of what these new arrivals see are people addicted to drugs, alcohol, and prostitution. It takes about three to five years before one can be fully integrated into Canadian society. For kids, that is too long a time to shield them from any destructive habits.

Worse still when refugees come to Winnipeg, they find other people from same countries who came under the same circumstances, and together form a community within the inner-city, creating a comfort but not necessarily a secure zone. In the meantime, the kids develop associates in the neighborhood who entice them to get involved. And unless there is a buffer or some good programs, when the kids get involved, it is in destructive behavior, and sometimes, it can be to the point where it becomes difficult, though not necessarily impossible, to redeem them. Speaking to the Winnipeg Free Press, the father of the boy who died said, "He was a good boy, we got along, but I could not tell him anything anymore." And there are many parents who, unfortunately, say the same. Nevertheless, is there anything the community can learn from what happened this week?

*Where to live in Winnipeg*

When refugees come to Winnipeg what is best for them? Somehow the onus to open the eyes and the minds of the new refugee arrivals is on those who are already here in Winnipeg. And for refugees from Africa, the onus is on the Africans who are already here to advise and help new arrivals. Advice must include where to live to be in a secure environment, what to do to learn about Canada and receive education that would allow you to jump start yourself into gainful employment. I am aware that certain things are easier said than done. But recognizing my role, I will do what I have the passion to do and am committed to doing, that is, inform and educate.

*Need for own community programs*

It is also important for communities, particularly the African community to have its own programs. I believe that the idea to build the African centre is the best idea so far on the table. But I also believe in virtual reality. The African community does not need to have a physical building to provide some of the needed help that new arrivals and the youths need. Those who are committed to helping young people or providing programs such as language training, counseling, etc. can still start now. If people cannot come forward and provide help when it is needed, chances are they will not be there even when the building is up.

At the funeral of the boy, one person shocked me when he said during our discourse, "I am not angry at the person who pulled the trigger on this boy, but I am angry at the lack of leadership by people in the community." What he meant was there are people out there who need to be doing something to help new arrivals such as this family and the youths such as the late boy, but they are not doing it. When are we going to do it? There is need for you to be involved. What can you do? Start doing it now?

*Managing risk*

The family of the boy decided to take the boys body back to Eritrea, Africa. The estimated cost is $10,000 and that is without accompaniment. It is astronomical and for most unaffordable. The family has to rely on community support. Everyone, however, can learn from this experience. Those who are here as well as new arrivals must be acquainted to available risk management strategies. One such strategy is having insurance.

You might have no control over losses suffered at home for which you need to travel. But for losses suffered here having sudden loss or life insurance can be key to alleviating difficulties in times of tragedy. For most new arrivals, perhaps insurance is a far distant thought. But hopefully, those in the profession will be quick to acquaint new arrivals to the need for life insurance. And friends and relatives who know the value of life insurance should be instrumental in driving the point home, so to say.

*The value of the community*

What would a family facing tragedy do, if it were not for the blessing of community? In my early civics classes, I learned the definition of government as "government of the people, for the people and by the people." Today, I believe this definition can be applied to the community as well. The community is of the people, for the people and by the people.

Knowing and understanding your community is important. You may not know its value until you are in need. How nice it would be for all to tear down walls and join together as a solid community. It is a wonderful experience when the community comes out together to help a family in need. This time, the horn of Africa community came out to help the grieving Eritrean family.

Truth is any community is larger than anyone member. Next time, the community may come to help you. Knowing the value of community, while you still have time, what can you do for your community? Whatever you think you can do, start and do it now. Yes, it is true. You and I can do better for new arrivals, for refugees, for youths and for everyone. TwCN.

# It's School Time! What Are You Planning To Study This School Year?

You could see it from the shops to the streets leading to schools. Both kids and parents busy shopping for school supplies. Buying everything including books, shoes, bags and whatever is on the kids' supply lists.

My wife and I had our turn. We took out our three boys and did like every other parent did for their kids - shopped according to the school supplies lists. It is costly, but the encouraging thing is that we had our kids excited for school.

Having grown up in Africa and remembering how my parents struggled to ensure I had a chance at school, I couldn't help it but remember those old days. Here my kids' supply lists asked for such items as 6 erasers, 20 pencils, 5 sticks of glue, etc. I couldn't help but to chuckle to myself. Chuckle because back in our days I could have one eraser and cut it in half and share with my brother or sister. If I had a pencil with an eraser that probably was sufficient. I don't remember having glue to myself alone. We sat about 4 to 6 kids per table. And we all used one bottle or one stick of glue at the table. We shared. And it never dawned on me that I was lacking something. I am, of course, aware that there were some whose parents were much better-off, and could provide them with all that they needed.

For most kids, going to school is a given. And most of them know what they are going to study. What about the parents? Three weeks ago, I had the opportunity to spend time with a brother from Sudan. The brother shared with me how his daughter, who has just reached the age of majority, decided to be on her on. And this wasn't without her first taking the dad (my friend) on a roller coaster ride with the police and child services. The girl went on her own for a little while. But within a year she was back with a totally new attitude toward her dad and life. She had just discovered that it was not that rosy out there. When my brother and I arrived at his home, I couldn't believe seeing this nineteen year old walking about the house so excited and exclaiming, "Baba you are back, nice to see you baba. Can I make you something, baba!" "What a charming girl!" I thought.

The dad allowed me to speak to her daughter. I discovered she had not even completed Grade 12. I advised her to go back to school immediately and complete Grade 12. Her ambition is to have her own business, which is a great ambition. But when you seriously think about it, you can't help but to ask, how can one, being a minority for that matter, manage a business in Canada without even a Grade 12 diploma? No business knowledge, no management knowledge, no banking knowledge. What are the chances to succeed? I will leave you to answer the question. Anyway, I got her attention. And I hope she will follow through on her promise.

My friend's daughter may not be the only one. There are many coming out of Africa and elsewhere to Canada, some as refugees, who need to improve their education. I would strongly encourage those who had no opportunity to complete Grade 12 before coming to Canada to do so here. There may be many doors to opportunities. But education, I believe, is the most common and reliable avenue that opens doors to unlimited opportunities.

There may be those who already have Grade 12 diplomas, but have no college training. Well, it's never too late in our country to receive a college diploma. You can work, and simultaneously enroll in the continuing education program at a college or university.

In Winnipeg, Canada, you can enroll at Red River Community College, or University of Winnipeg or University of Manitoba Continuing Education Faculties. The challenge, perhaps, is choosing the field of study to focus on. And that depends on your aptitude and career interest. Seeking advice from those who have walked the same path before may not be a bad idea. And hopefully whoever provides you advice will have your interest at heart and be objective enough in advising you.

All some people might need is improving their language skills. If they know French, they may plan to learn English, and vice versa. Improving oral and written communication skills could be the key to getting your dream job, or succeeding in your entrepreneurship.

What about those with college diplomas and university degrees? Is there room for improvement? I strongly believe that yes, there is room for improvement. You may not go back to college or university, but you can do your studies through your professional body or staff training department at your work. Even myself as I write, I have three courses lined up for me to take this fall. By so doing I hope, like all other graduates, to improve my professional competitive advantage and come up-to-date with cutting edge knowledge in my area of work.

Education or training is not without critics. There are those who believe you don't necessarily need education to make it in Canada. But as it is in advanced democracies, you simply have to respect their point of view. All in all, you have to make your own judgment as to what is really good for you and your family. The fact is, for those who have made it in this society; it is easier for them to help those who have attained decent education than those who have none. Being a new comer to this country, if you are not eager to receive education, you are taking a chance at committing yourself to a helpless life.

Like all dreams, going back to school can be challenging. There is the issue of money, the issue of parenting, and the demands from home. There is a lot to contend with. But where there is a will there is a way. And some dreams do take time to be achieved. Fortunately, the secret to achieving dreams or ambitions is not money or time as some people may make you believe, rather it is your will. And I hope you have a strong will for pursuing your personal development through training this year.

There is also the challenge of the subject matter itself. Some people may experience difficulties cracking some courses. I believe this is where your community network must come in. Find people who are walking the same path, or who have been there before. See if they can help you in anyway. Sometimes, it takes a second teacher to help you understand the subject matter.

Often, people make a mistake of thinking they are alone, when in fact they are not. If you choose to be alone, yes you will be alone. And if you choose to have friends, yes you will have them. My advice is, choose to walk a just and fair path in life, love and respect yourself and your friends, and you will always have friends. I believe that your friends will take an extra mile and eagerly help you get the necessary training and find a better job than you currently have. As no man is an island, be open minded and, if possible, make use of your community and its resources.

Finally, I wish to end by reminding you, in the words of H. Jackson Brown, Jr. that just the moment you say "I give up," someone else seeing the same situation is saying "My, what a great opportunity." No doubt, the beginning of every school year is an opportunity to further personal development through training and education. TwCN.

# African-Canadian Community System for Support, Integration and Networking - Part 1

As individual Africans we all have our needs which, when put together, we could call our African community needs. Notwithstanding the scientific ways to classify needs, I believe our needs can be classified based on how they are fulfilled. There are some needs that are met by public services or the three-levels of government. There are other needs that are met by private services or profit businesses. Yet still, there are those needs that are nither met by public nor private sectors. It is the latter category of needs that is the reason for many African community organized not-for-profit associations.

Most not-for-profit associations are formed with good intentions, but arguably these organizations don't quite get to fully satisfy the needs of their members. Could it be that the effectiveness of non-profit organizations depends on how they are positioned in the community and linked to other community organizations to help leverage resources in the process of meeting members needs? Or could it be that organizations are formed, but never really work to develop processes through which members' needs may be satisfied?

Chrispin Ntungo

## Understanding our new society

Your body and mine are wonderfully and fearfully made. Science reviews that our bodies are made up of systems. There is, to name a few, the digestive system, the respiratory system, the nervous system, the reproductive system, etc. For each system to function successfully, all of its components must be properly functional and linked. For instance for the digestive system to function properly, the mouth, the esophagus, the stomach and the intestines, etc must be health and orderly linked and perform their functions successfully.

Similarly, the Canadian society is like a body. It is made up of several multicultural groups, synonymous to the body's systems. Those multicultural groups that have properly functioning and well linked parts appear to do better on average than other groups. Such multicultural groups as the Greek-Canadians, Italian-Canadians, Israeli-Canadians, etc. have established and linked varied community components that take care of members identified needs within their communities. What could all this mean for a community such as the African community in Manitoba?

## Reality for the African community

African-Canadians (meaning new arrivals and those who have been here many years) need to understand the system they come into in order to successfully live here. This understanding includes the recognition that Canada is a multicultural society, implying that different ethnic or cultural communities of immigrants co-exist. Each community works to preserve and celebrate its culture while at the same time appreciates the other communities' ethnicity and culture. Even more important is that each community works to fulfill its member's needs.

All Canadians have equal rights before the law. For this reason, the Canadian society is such that the government is responsible for providing public services to all Canadians without prejudice. And the Canadian society is such that services that are not provided by the government are provided by the private sector. If there are still other needs that are not fulfilled by the public or the private sectors, this is where individual communities are at liberty to provide specialized services or programs and activities to meet the needs of their members. Particularly important is the need to enhance the integration of new arrivals into the community as well as to keep the community together so it can grow and prosper. And often the challenge is how to successfully provide community based programs and services.

*Partial or complete integration*

For new arrivals into Canada it takes a while to understand Canada and her community systems. Of much interest is the fact that new African arrivals have to integrate themselves into the Canadian system. The success and the extent of integration into the system often depend on age and the person's ability to relate to Canadians.

Those who succeed at integration, succeed at integrating into one or two aspects of the Canadian society (partial integration), but rarely does it happen that a person comfortably integrates into all aspects of the Canadian society (complete integration). And this is one reason why for some people the established system fails to fully meet their needs. When this happens the individuals fall out of the mainstream system and risk to be misfits.

The impact of this experience is much serious on young people. Consequences include unhealthy cultural shock, kids taking to inappropriate behavior, rebelling and finding themselves in the hands of law enforcement agents. And those who have successfully integrated into the system can't help, but ask: "Can the community play any role to alleviate the problem or help minimize the undesirable impact?" Fortunately, most Africans say, "Yes" to this question.

In the past, and even presently, Africans have tried to fill the void through individual associations. But somehow, the dream of meeting people's needs through associations is not fully achieved. There are many reasons why. It would take another edition of TwCN to do justice presenting them.

*Confronting reality with solutions*

To cut the long story short, I am one of those in the community who are truly convinced that unless Africans unleash the zeal, passion, talents and expertise that individual Africans and the collective community have, the African community will continue to spin wheels for many years to come. I am one of those in the community who are confident that with strong leadership, and personal commitment of every African to making a difference amongst fellow Africans, Africans can achieve unprecedented success and prosperity in Manitoba.

I am also one of those in the community who strongly believe that change, and effective change for that matter, will only come if the African community recognizes that Canada is a society of community systems and adopt a systems approach to managing its challenges. The system could be conceptualized, organized, drawn, understood, shared and implemented by Africans. The system components can include both African community based and public and private initiatives.

Of prime importance is to have community programs in the system solely coordinated by the Africans themselves. However, in order to develop a solid African community system in Manitoba it is first important to understand what comprises the Manitoba African community.

*Make-up of the Manitoba African Community*

At the grassroots, the Manitoba African community consists of individuals and families. Some of these individuals and families are African-Canadians, some are landed immigrants, some are visa employees and others are visa students or visitors. Often individuals and families from the same African country organize themselves and form an association and elect leaders.

Leaders come together in form of an African community leaders' committee formally organized as the African Communities of Manitoba Inc (ACOMI.) The goal of ACOMI is to bring all Africans in Manitoba under one house, formally organized as the African-Canadian Cultural and Heritage Centre, Inc (ACCHCI).

In addition, there are Africans who are enterprising or entrepreneurial who organize their own private businesses or non-government organizations (NGOs). As expected, private businesses hope to have Africans patronize their businesses. NGO's work to meet the needs of special segments of the African-Canadian community in Manitoba or internationally and nationally. As you can see it is quite a complex community structure.

Other than the individuals, all African community organizations are formed with the common goal of serving and meeting those needs of individual Africans in Manitoba that are not met by services provided by the public or private organizations. In order to effectively meet the needs of individuals, community organizations must tailor their programs and services so as to complement government and private services. The challenge is how do these African organizations achieve their goals effectively? Can these goals be effectively achieved in isolation or as part of the complete whole – the African-Canadian community system?

*In anticipation*

Next edition of TwCN shows how the Manitoba African community could put these components of the community together and form an effective and efficient community system for support, integration and networking. The community system would provide services, including programs and activities, to satisfy the unfulfilled needs of all the members of the African community. And to really benefit from the system, every African – whether young or old - would need to be part of the system. TwCN.

# African-Canadian Community System for Support, Integration and Networking - Part 2

W hen people say, "In Africa it takes a village to raise a child," one may wonder what they mean. Well, its easy to see the meaning. They are talking about having a system in which a child is raised. And in an African village, they are talking about a system of uncles, aunties, grandparents, brothers and sisters, etc. These people who are part of the African Village System play their own significant supportive roles in the process of raising an African child. Believe me or not, the African community here equally needs a system in which to bring up children as well as to support one another for easy integration of new comers and networking with each other and the larger community.

In order to successfully reach the individual members of the community and provide services that will meet or exceed their expectations, the African community needs to design and implement a system linking and coordinating all organizations and processes in place for providing necessary services. A depiction of one such system is provided at the end of this article in Figure 1.

*Services and organizations*

Last week, TwCN enjoyed the liberty and helped classify community needs into three groups. First, those needs met by public services.

Secondly, those needs met by private services providers, and thirdly, those needs that may be met by the community itself.

Public services include such services as child services, citizenship and immigration, schools and colleges, employment, family services, health, police, and start-up housing, etcetera. Private services include accounting services, banking, business consulting, financial planning, insurance, legal services, real estate services and computer services, etcetera. The services not covered by public and private services providers would be provided by non-profit community organizations. These services include community sports, cultural programs, education and career counseling, minority employment strategies, family counseling, housing strategies, immigration strategies, investment clubs, new immigrant counseling and youth counseling, etcetera.

In order to fulfill all these needs within and for the African community, there is need for the community to deliberately have a system of organizations and businesses. Given the nature of services, the organizations may include government departments to provide public services, private companies to provide private services, and community organizations to provide community services.

As a matter of fact, government departments are already available. All the community needs to do is know how to access them. And the African community has some already existing organizations. To this end the African community appears to be well equipped to provide the necessary community services.

To name a few, organized African Community organizations are such associations as Nigerian Association of Manitoba, Southern African Association of Manitoba, Sudanese Association of Manitoba, Ghanaian Union, Ugandan-Canadian Association of Manitoba, and many others. Like indicated in the last edition, such organizations are led by leaders who represent their organizations at the African Communities of Manitoba Inc (ACOMI), which is the umbrella organization uniting all country or region based organizations. In principle, the home for African individuals and their respective associations is the venue of activities and programs called the African Canadian Cultural and Heritage Centre, Inc. (ACCHCI).

In addition, the community has non-government organizations or NGOs, which include such organizations as African Canadian Disability Community Association (ACDCA), International African Child and Peace Foundation of Canada (IACPFC), Sudanese Relief and Rehabilitation Program (SRRP), and private businesses which can provide services to individuals and families in the community.

Furthermore, our community has a working virtual office called the African Community of Manitoba Secretariat, which by function serves as a coordinating and communications facility owned and operated by the African Communities of Manitoba Inc. Its function is to provide essential communication services to the community as a whole. It still remains to be seen to see African leaders understand their community system and then find a way to properly coordinate these organizations and have them work together to achieve their common goal of fully meeting the African community needs.

*Programs and Activities*

Programs and activities include any initiatives spearheaded or implemented by community associations, the three levels of government, African-Canadian NGOs and, professional and private businesses.

In principle, community programs and activities could be provided from the African Canadian Cultural and Heritage Centre. In the absence of the physical building, programs can be provided on satelite sites around the city. All that the African-Canadians in Winnipeg need is a print out of a quarterly or annual schedule. The schedule can indicate the dates, time and places where the program or activity is taking place. People can register or simply drop in to participate. As long as you know the majority of the people in attendance will be fellow Africans, it would be better to attend. Programs can be during the week or on weekends, as well as during the day or in the evenings.

*Could there be challenges?*

Like every worthwhile undertaking has challenges, establishing an effective community system is not without its own challenges. Here are some of the challenges, the community must expect.

**Program and activity coordinators.** Finding Program and Activity Coordinators may be a challenge. This is where everyone's commitment, dedication, passion, zeal, or leadership is needed.

**Low participation from community members.** Low participation can be discouraging. That is why, when you do something, you must do it because you like it. If so many people don't show up, can you still go ahead and just enjoy yourself? Hopefully, the community will be doing enough to promote its own programs and people will be continually interested.

**Community system maintenance costs.** Like every system, it costs money to maintain a system. Let us not think that we can fulfill all our community needs for free. We must be prepared to pay nominal fees to cover operational costs. That means you may need to pay a registration fee for some programs or activities or a user fee for some activities.

Community members must be willing to pay nominal fees in order for the system to survive. If you can't be willing to pay anything, you can as well forget about your dreams for the African community. If indeed the benefit is to help our kids to be together, to help new comers integrate easily into the community, to live as a community, to enjoy each other's company, etc. then whatever it may cost to maintain and sustain the system must be justifiable.

*Overcoming challenges and making it work*

Moreover, it is important that each and every African in Manitoba see themselves as part of the system. Whether young or old, you must see yourself somewhere within the system. You can see yourself as a new comer, an individual, a leader, a participant in a community program, a youth on training, a seeker of government services, a professional or business owner, etcetera. And wherever you are in the system, just remember to do your part. Be willing to help those you see need help. Seek help when and if you think you need it.

To make the calendar work, the community needs to have a schedule and assign responsibility to execute certain programs and activities to committees of community leaders. For example, if you need to put up an educational seminar for the youth, assign such an activity to a committee of three or four organization leaders. These can be SAAM, UCAM and Ethiopia for instance. An activity such as Africa in the Park can be assigned to three or four community leaders such as Ghana, SAAM and Nigeria. It can then be emphasized that it is the responsibility of all other community leaders to see to it that there people participate.

In the meantime, the Secretariat will do its part to announce the event to the community. I am one of those in the community who believe that if we create awareness of community needs, promote the benefits of community services and the significance of working together as part of the system, we can achieve whatever we dream to achieve for the African community.

The outsiders may be asking, "Shall they really work together?" And we need to show that yes, the African community has people who can work together. The idea of each association struggling to make it happen alone, is working too much for so little. Collaboration, teamwork, and community spirit is what will cause us to be effective and efficient and, successful and prosperous as a community as well as individuals.

I am sure you would love to hear more and I am thankful for that. But I am done. TwCN.

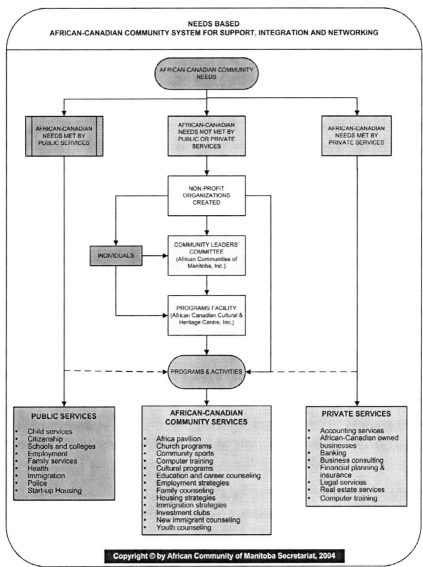

Figure 1.

# African-Canadian Community System for Support, Integration and Networking - Part 3

Welcoming me into his office, Mr. Paul Shawa, LLB. from the community asked: "How is the Secretariat? It has never been done so well before." "Yeah, just trying to do what I can," I replied while making myself comfortable in his client seat. I couldn't say more, because deep in me there is a desire to do even better. But "how?" is the question. And this reminds me of Dr. Trust Beta's words in one of our community leader's meetings where she said, "Everyone is busy trying to find means to pay bills." There is lots of truth in her statement.

"What motivates you?" is a common interview question asked those attending employment interviews or reviews. And to be able to get a job, you better do your homework and answer this question truthfully. Many of Africans in the community ask, "What motivates a man to run a facility as well as he does and for free." Well if you are reading this, you are a great person. Perhaps you don't know it. Believe you me, you are. It's great and important people like you that keep me going. And because you are great and important, I have to do my job right to serve you better.

The last two editions of TwCN focused on African-Canadian Community System for Integration, Support and Networking. I hope you are not bored reading this stuff. I am impressed to serve

180

the community thoroughly well. And that begins with making the "how to" process pretty clear. I hope this edition of TwCN does just that – makes the process for integration, support and networking pretty clear.

*Process for African Canadian community system for support, integration and networking*

This documentation allows every African community member to read from the same page, understand and work within the same system, thereby contribute to efforts for attaining and maintaining community unity, support and prosperity.

# 1. SYSTEM DESCRIPTION

| | |
|---|---|
| COMMUNITY | African Community |
| SYSTEM NAME | African-Canadian Community System for Support, Integration and Networking |
| SYSTEM MANAGER | African Communities of Manitoba Inc |
| SYSTEM EXPERT | African Community of Manitoba Secretariat |

SYSTEM GOALS

1. To provide supportive and networking opportunities to African community members including children, youth, and adults

2. To facilitate new comer integration into the African-Canadian and the Canadian communities

SYSTEM INPUT(S)

• African individuals in need of peer support, community support, community activities, employment, youth activities, professional assistance, etc.

• Individuals and families in need of African family activities, community fun, cultural expression, etc.

INPUT SUPPLIERS

• Canadian immigration and citizenship
• African community families

SYSTEM OUTPUT(S)

• Successful and prosperous African individuals and families
• United and prosperous African community

SYSTEM CUSTOMER(S)

African community members, including
• African-Canadians and/or
• New immigrants
• Visa students
• Youths
• Families
• Refugees, etc.

## 3. SYSTEM HELPING STEPS AND ACTIVITIES

| STEP | ACTIVITY or ACTION | PERFORMER | GOAL |
| --- | --- | --- | --- |
| 1. | Welcome new African(s) who arrive:<br>• immigrants,<br>• visa students,<br>• refugees, etc. | • Host families<br>• Welcome Place<br>• International Centre<br>• Family members<br>• Friends<br>• Others | Beginning new life in a new place. |
| 2. | Provide orientation to new arrival or individual | • Host families<br>• Welcome Place<br>• International Centre<br>• Family members<br>• Friends<br>• Others | Orientation |
| 3. | Introduce new arrival to their country or regional association or the African Community of Manitoba Secretariat. | • Host families<br>• Welcome Place<br>• International Centre<br>• Family members<br>• Friends<br>• Others | Integration |
| 4. | Add individual to country or regional association members list and include phone number. | Association President/ Secretary | Acceptance |
| 5. | Does new arrival have e-mail address?<br><br>If Yes, go to Step 6<br>If No, maintain Step 4 | • Association President or Secretary or other<br>• Family members<br>• Friends | |

183

| STEP | ACTIVITY or ACTION | PERFORMER | GOAL |
|---|---|---|---|
| 6. | Introduce new arrival to the African Community of Manitoba Secretariat by e-mail and provide individual's e-mail address. | • Association President or Secretary or other<br>• Family members<br>• Friends | Integration and communication |
| 7. | Add new arrival to African community communication list | African community Secretariat | Communication loop |
| 8. | Send information about the African community organization to the new arrival. | African Community Secretariat | Introduction/ Orientation |
| 9. | Invite new arrival to African Community programs or activities | • Association President or Secretary or other<br>• Family members<br>• Friends<br>• African Community Secretariat | Integration |
| 10. | Does the individual need assistance with:<br>• Employment?<br>• Immigration?<br>• Child services?<br>• Family services?<br>• Citizenship?<br>• Start-up Housing?<br>• Education?<br><br>If Yes, proceed to Step 11<br>If No, go to Step 12 | • Association President or Secretary or other<br>• Family members<br>• Friends<br>• Host family<br>• African Community Secretariat<br>• Welcome place | Finding ways to help |

| STEP | ACTIVITY or ACTION | PERFORMER | GOAL |
|------|--------------------|-----------|------|
| 11. | Help the new arrival get assistance from the appropriate government office.<br>• If you don't know the right office contact the African Community Secretariat or your community leader for assistance. | • Association President or Secretary or other<br>• Family members<br>• Friends<br>• Host family<br>• African Community Secretariat<br>• Welcome place | Support and assistance |
| 12. | Does the new arrival or individual need to be involved with community programs such as:<br>• Employment strategies?<br>• Immigration strategies?<br>• Youth counseling?<br>• Community sports?<br>• Family counseling?<br>• Housing strategies?<br>• Education and career counseling?<br>• Cultural programs?<br>• Church programs?<br>• New immigrant counseling?<br>• Investment clubs?<br>• Computer training?<br><br>If Yes, proceed to Step 13<br>If No, go to Step 14 | • Association President or Secretary or other<br>• Family members<br>• Friends<br>• Host family<br>• African Community Secretariat<br>• Welcome place | Finding out how to help |

| STEP | ACTIVITY or ACTION | PERFORMER | GOAL |
|---|---|---|---|
| 13. | Advise the individual and/or direct them to the **Community Program or Activity Coordinator** – see directory or inquire with the African Community Secretariat | • Association President or Secretary or other<br>• Family members<br>• Friends<br>• Host family<br>• Welcome place | Support for integration |
| 14. | Does the new arrival or individual need professional help with:<br>• Legal services?<br>• Public health services?<br>• Accounting services?<br>• Business start-up?<br>• Financial planning and/or insurance?<br>• Real estate services?<br><br>If Yes, go to Step 15<br>If No, go to Step 16 | • Association President or Secretary or other<br>• Family members<br>• Friends<br>• Host family<br>• African Community Secretariat<br>• Welcome place | Professional support within the community |
| 15. | Advise the individual and direct them to the **Community Professional** who provides requested services. | • Association President or Secretary or other<br>• Family members<br>• Friends<br>• Host family<br>• African Community Secretariat<br>• Welcome place | Support and assistance. |

| STEP | ACTIVITY or ACTION | PERFORMER | GOAL |
|---|---|---|---|
| 16. | Does the individual need other services such as:<br>• Religious?<br>• Disability?<br>• Relief?<br>• General advice? etc.<br>If Yes, proceed to Step 17<br>If No, go to Step 18 | • Association President or Secretary or other<br>• Family members<br>• Friends<br>• Host family<br>• African Community Secretariat<br>• Welcome place | Finding out special needs |
| 17. | Advise and direct them to an appropriate NGO specializing in providing requested services<br>Examples:<br>• International African Child Relief and Peace Foundation<br>• African-Canadian Disability Community Association<br>• Immigrant Women's Association of Manitoba<br>• Immigrant Women's Counseling Services<br>• Church, etc. | • Association President or Secretary or other<br>• Family members<br>• Friends<br>• Host family<br>• African Community Secretariat<br>• Welcome place | Support |

| STEP | ACTIVITY or ACTION | PERFORMER | GOAL |
|------|--------------------|-----------|------|
| 18. | Does the individual want to be active in the community?<br><br>If Yes, go to Step 19<br>If No, go to Step 20 | • Association President or Secretary or other<br>• Family members<br>• Friends<br>• Host family<br>• African Community Secretariat<br>• Welcome place | Finding out networking interests |
| 19 | Direct them to the appropriate association or community programs:<br>• African Communities of Manitoba, Inc.<br>• Africa Pavilion<br>• African-Canadian Disability Community Association, etc. | • Association President or Secretary or other<br>• Family members<br>• Friends<br>• African Community Secretariat | Networking opportunities |
| 20 | Does the individual feel comfortable?<br><br>If Yes, go to Step 21<br>If No, go to Step 22 | • Association President or Secretary or other<br>• Family members<br>• Friends | Finding out if they feel supported and integrated |
| 21 | • Encourage them to get involved<br>• Tell them you are happy to see they are so well integrated. | • Family members<br>• Friends | Support |

| STEP | ACTIVITY or ACTION | PERFORMER | GOAL |
|------|--------------------|-----------|------|
| 22 | • Find out what is it that interests the individual.<br>• If you notice a problem, advise them against involvement in inappropriate activities.<br>• If possible inform community leaders. | • Family members<br>• Friends | Support |

If all of us, or is it most of us? could make the right decisions, and love our community and live united, we would improve our chances to prosper as a community. The future may be too distant from now to see the fruits, but we can trust that all our efforts will pay off in and for our children.

*What about African community values?*

Are you a visible minority of African decent? Imagine what you would be like if you believed and lived your life according to the following community values:

1. Availability for programs and activities
2. Commitment to community initiatives
3. Communication so we are all informed
4. Competence in whatever we do
5. Concern for one another
6. Consistence in action and activity
7. Courtesy for one another and others
8. Flexibility with one another
9. Friendliness with one another
10. Helpfulness
11. Integrity in all our community and business relations
12. Responsiveness to the needs of others
13. Security in numbers
14. Timeliness in everything we do

If you were in my class I would teach you about these values, and hope that you will remember to live by them; not because you have to write an exam at the end of the course, but because you love them. However, you are not in my class. The best I can do now is to tell you what I believe. I am one of those who believe that if you do, you will be of much benefit to both the community and your family. But I also believe as the adage says, "You can take a horse to the river, but you cannot force it to drink the water." I trust you will. TwCN.

# The Looming Identity Crisis

One question that everyone encounters every now and then is "Where did you come from?" This is particularly true for those in Canada. And when encountered it makes one ask "But why ask me this question?" Often for the person being asked there is a feeling of being noticeably different from everyone else in the Canadian society. They feel like they somehow don't quite belong. So in response, people struggle with the answer.

Deep down in the heart, so to say, they want the person asking to obviously appreciate that they are here and that is what is important. So it is unnecessary to ask the "where did you come from" question. "You mean you cannot see; I can be Canadian? or that I am Canadian," often the thought goes. "People like me can't be from here?" "That is a ridiculous question." And often the answer is retaliatory, and what about you, where do you come from? - a somehow satisfying and fair response under the circumstances. The core issue behind the "where do you come from?" question is identity of the roots. And I hope there is no identity crisis for many coming out of Africa.

*Whatever happened to the word Negro*

Once black people in America were called Negros, and still, like all blacks, they are. But during the slave trade the word Negro was so much misused to demean blacks and for that reason no one wanted to be called Negro. You see the word Negro is on the same plane as "Caucasian" or "Oriental" words used to refer to Europeans and Asians. As a solution the black people in America adopted the term "African American." And it is a suitable word as long as it is applied to those blacks in America. What about those blacks outside America and outside Africa. What should we and our children be called?

*Motherland Africa speaks out*

We wouldn't know what we should be called unless we ask mother Africa to name us. TwCN did just that mid September 2004. And here is what mother Africa says:

"My children, I am happy to be in touch with you. I have had mixed feelings to see you all leave me and go to overseas. On one hand, I have been happy because I know you have gone to enjoy freedom and peace; you have gone to pursue dreams so you can prosper.

On the other hand, I have been worried because you have gone and become known as Americans, British, Canadians, Australians and others. I am not truly convinced you are that. I see a looming identity crisis. Would you now listen to me? Heed my word for once. I would like to call you Overseas Africans. It does not matter where you are in Arabia, United Kingdom, Germany, France, United States, Canada, Australia, world all over; you are still my beloved African children. Call yourselves and your children Overseas Africans.

Everyday that passes; I wish I had the opportunity you have. But unfortunately your father, even the African leader, continues to deny your brethren and myself freedom and peace, and opportunities to prosper. Daily, I am forced to swallow the blood and/or the remains of your brethren being killed by ruthless warlords. I am tired. So don't be surprised when you see more of your brothers and sisters coming to join you. Please welcome them and help them to settle so they can also enjoy peace and freedom and have the opportunity to prosper.

Finally, I implore you to be part of your brother's work. I have impressed your brother to start publishing Overseas African Magazine which I believe will help to keep you together, will help preserve your heritage, and will help teach your children African values. Through Overseas African Magazine you will share your experiences, including your dreams, challenges and accomplishments. And by so doing I will inspire, motivate and empower you and your children to succeed and prosper overseas.

Now keep your peace and enjoy your freedom and don't forget about your brothers and sisters who are still with me." Sincerely, even I, your motherland Africa.

To honor its readers, TwCN has reserved December 16, 2004 issue for readers' stories. Tell how you think TwCN has benefited you and others. A number of impressive stories will be included in the 52nd edition of TwCN which will be published on December 16, 2004. And thank you very much for being there and for your support. TwCN.

# The Secret of America's Mighty

I f you are open minded and mindful of the welfare of your people, at the very least, you can't help it but admire the United States of America's presidential debate. Listening to the American presidential candidates debate, is a rare opportunity for learning about democracy, learning about values, learning about conviction, learning about faith, learning about building bridges and learning about what to value in your personal life.

It has been interesting to watch George W. Bush and Kerry Edwards battle it out in the presidential debates leading up to American presidential elections on November 2, 2004. But does it matter what the American presidential candidates debate on? Does it matter who finally ends up in the White House?

It is human nature to take sides. When you take sides, you follow the debate closely and subsequent analysis by the media. You feel affected. You feel scratched on one side or the other. Inevitably you want to wish victory for one of the two candidates. In this sense you would say it matters what American presidential candidates debate. But the irony is that unless you are an american you have no control, you are just an outsider looking in.

What do you do when there are certain things about either candidate that you like? You know that the White House can only take one president. It is at this point that you start thinking, "it does not matter who finally ends up in the White House." Whether the democrat or the republican ends up in the White House, for many of us it will still be the same old world. We will still face the same challenges we have known over the years.

What then is the value of American presidential debate to those of us outside America, and especially those coming out of Africa? During the debate, you couldn't help but admire the clarity in identifying issues to debate on. Such issues as education, jobs, health, immigration, environment, etc. You couldn't help but admire the fearlessness of the candidates. Candidates debated while being sure that after the debate they would go home safe and secure without fear of being harassed by any elements of the opposition. Candidates debated believing that the campaign playing field was level and that the election process was transparent.

At the end of the debate, you couldn't help but to admire how the candidates shook their hands. You couldn't help but to admire how the two candidates hugged each other's wife. You couldn't help but to admire how the candidates were surrounded by their families with no ill feelings from the audience. And You couldn't help but to ask, "Why can't other societies, especially those in Africa do the same?" America, indeed, has something to offer the world. Arguably not everything, but sure America leads when it comes to tolerance, peace and freedom. America could be and is a school for many who dream to be free and prosperous. But who would learn from America when what comes to mind first is meanness towards her.

It appears that the secret of America's mighty lies not in what people know America for – wealth, money, movies and a powerful military, but rather in the ability of leaders and their followers with opposing views to respect their differences, tolerate one another, unite in peace and freedom and fight the common enemy. And the common enemy is not one armed with weapons of war; rather it is hunger, disease, poverty, unemployment, and illiteracy. America has long defeated the common enemy. Consequently, freedom and prosperity have followed. It is this freedom and prosperity that attracts people to America.

Everytime you see opportunities for improvement, your heart must go out to Africa and her people. You see, the people of Africa have so much in form of dreams. But Africans still have to overcome the common enemy. This may not happen until African leaders have renewed minds and learn from the American school to practice the values of tolerance of opposing views, respect for independent opinion, and promote peace and freedom for their people.

Lastly, it does not hurt to make you know that over the years, one of the hardest things we have learned at TwCN is to give credit where it is due. And we have learned, though some may argue otherwise, that for certain things America deserves credit. TwCN.

# Your Money Adds Up to US$45 Billion a Year, Wow!

Recently, TwCN had the opportunity to review the *"How Africa is courting its exiles"* article by Elizabeth Blunt of BBC News (2004/10/17), courtesy of David Binding. It was a mind opener. Most importantly, Blunt's article touches on issues that any Overseas African can't help but be pleased to see discussed. It is for this reason that this edition of TwCN is dedicated to shedding more light on the issues raised.

Blunt begins her article by saying:

*"On the fringes of the European Social Forum in London, people of African descent are holding their own conference - and discussing how Africa could benefit from their achievements. Suddenly Africa is wooing its exiles."*

I hope that Overseas Africans will not always feel as if they live on the fringes of overseas societies. Overseas Africans must always strive for integration with respective overseas societies, be it in the UK, France, Canada, US or Australia, etc. At least Canada recognizes this fact and that is why the government has a policy on multiculturalism. In this day and age, the multiculturalism policy benefits not only Africans but other ethnic communities as well. It's a policy that recognizes diversity and equality of all people on the face of the Globe.

Addressing the idea of how Africa could benefit from the achievements of Overseas Africans is interesting. There is no doubt that even presently Africa benefits from Overseas African achievements. What is lacking, however, is a formal recognition of this benefit by some

African governments. It's all about motivation and appreciation. A formal recognition warranting discussion in African parliaments could go a long way motivating Overseas Africans to send even more of their hard earned money and make plans for some solid investments.

Blunt continues to write saying:

*"Some of the continent's best brains, and deepest pockets are in London, Paris or New York, not in Lagos or Nairobi. Add in all the people of African descent, black Americans, the population of the Caribbean and large parts of Brazil, and Africa has millions of prosperous and influential people potentially on its side."*

What a brilliant observation! You see, it is indisputable fact that Africa needs money for development. If losing its "best brains" is a problem for Africa, then the solution may lie in how to benefit from the monetary power assumed by Africa's "best brains and deepest pockets" and others who live abroad. Even more important, if African institutions (such as those for health and education) rather than families are to benefit from the wealth of Overseas Africans, Africans at home need to put in place a formal accountable channel. I believe the "best brains" within the Overseas African community can help devise such a channel – and could be a result of some worthy research.

Blunt also observes, *"When the new African Union was drawing up its constitution it made space for these people of African origin; after north, south, east west and central Africa, the diaspora was designated the sixth region of the continent."*

For the moment I feel that the African Union made a very important observation. This is what every African country is supposed to do. The minds of majority of first generation Overseas Africans are back home in Africa. You wonder why in recent years there has been so much innovation in telecommunications. The reason is because the wires are constantly engaged – overseas Africans communicating with their relatives in Africa.

Hearing that the African Union has an Ambassador in Geneva is great news. And as expected of most African women she made a great remark that Blunt appropriately penned down saying:

*"Sophie Kalinde, the African Union's ambassador in Geneva, is one of the links with this constituency in Europe. "It's a big population. You know that the dispersal of the population is such that Africa cannot ignore the presence of its own outside Africa.""*

Sounds like words of a caring African mother reflecting mother Africa's deep concern. I think that if African governments do not approve and are not willing to relate with Overseas Africans, then Overseas Africans, for the sake of their relatives and for the love of the motherland, can work with such an Ambassador of the African Union. Overseas Africans have enormous ideas to help advance development in Africa. These ideas can be shared through the African Union ambassadors.

Writing on money transfers, Blunt wrote:

*"Perhaps the real wake-up call came after 11 September, when governments began to make careful records of money movements. Best estimates suggest that Africans working abroad send home some $45bn a year. . . . But most of it goes on living expenses for their families; they are less likely than expatriate Indians for instance, to invest their savings back home in Africa."*

The initiative to track money transfers around the world is not an African initiative, but a western initiative. But thank goodness, African governments will get to know too.

Previously TwCN has alluded to the fact that most Overseas Africans are "philanthropists" in their own extended families. That implies they send money back home to support their relatives. It is not uncommon to find Overseas Africans in the valley of decision – to donate money to a charity overseas or to send money to family in Africa. More often than not, Overseas Africans decide to send money to family in Africa.

Previous to the events of 2001, no one had an idea how much money Overseas Africans send back to Africa. Now we have a possible "best estimate" at US$45 billion dollars a year. That is an enormous and unbelievable sum of money. I will have to wait a few more years and see more annual figures to believe. Nevertheless, if $45bn a year is true, then for sure Overseas Africans are collectively powerful. So powerful that with a little bit of mobilization, Overseas Africans can be a voice with which African governments can reckon.

Why are Overseas Africans less likely to invest their savings in Africa? Good observation and good question. Presently, majority of Overseas Africans experience a lot of problems working through relatives or friends to implement any projects at home. Often, the best projects Overseas Africans achieve are limited to building a house for themselves, parents or some other relatives. Even then the process is not without headaches. Often whoever is helping to coordinate a project at home fails to account for the money. The demands for the money are unending, but no results. In the end the sponsoring Overseas African gives up. And the only option for offering assistance ends up not being investment, but a hand to mouth phenomenon.

Further, I am one of those who liked how Kalinde put it when responding to another of Blunt's questions. She said, "*But if African governments want the diaspora's money, they will have to earn it.*" African governments are known for having corrupt leaderships whose part of their interest, when dealing with foreign money is how much can end up in their own accounts. Overseas Africans know them. Therefore, African governments will have to first demonstrate that they can channel the money and use it all for the intended purposes. They have to demonstrate that they are trustworthy and accountable.

Furthermore, Blunt wrote:

"*Another message to this meeting was that collectively Africans living abroad have real strength. If they want better governance, more transparency, a more stable investment climate, they should demand it; now they know the demands are backed by $45bn a year, their governments may be more ready to listen.*"

The question here is "how best can Overseas Africans demand *better governance, more transparency,* and *a more stable investment climate?*"

This is where the "best brains" need to be solicited. Likely, we need institutionalized Overseas African strength. One way Overseas Africans can achieve institutionalized strength is to form an Overseas African Bank and a competitor indeed to African Development Bank, the World Bank and the International Monetary Fund. An Overseas African Bank would operate in all African capital cities and have branches in London, Paris, New York, Toronto, etc. If this happened Overseas Africans would be pleased to deposit their money in such a bank, and the bank can in turn support development initiatives in Africa.

The shareholders of above named competitors are mostly western governments, including Canada. Overseas African bank would be owned by Overseas African individuals. Imagine $45bln in a bank you own and you are likely one of the directors. There is no doubt that you could use it to draw the attention of African governments and have them listen. Dreams are often sweeter than reality. And this one is, but not an impossible one! TwCN.

# Dreams

People from all over the world are motivated by different reasons to immigrate, particularly, to Canada and America. Most of the common reasons given are economic and political in nature. Generally, it appears that people come to North America, including Canada to seek economic prosperity, peace and freedom. Yes, these are general goals that people hold explicitly or implicitly. But do Africans ever earnestly pursue their specific goals when they adopt Canada or the United States as their land of prosperity, peace and freedom. The intent of this article is to remind African immigrants of their dreams and the need to pursue those dreams.

By speaking to people, I have come to realize that people have specific dreams. Some dream to have gainful employment, decent accommodation and to drive in order to consider themselves as successful. Others include in their dreams, happy family, good health, and to travel. And these are good goals. But they are basic dreams. At the very least, I would like to think of them as the foundation of even greater dreams.

I don't wish to simplify the process leading to prosperity. I know that for some people it may not be easy to attain even the least of these dreams. But this article should serve to encourage such. In order to be a successful community, dreams must go beyond the situation of simply managing to put food on the table. Putting food on the table is the equivalent of paying bills here in Canada. Immigrants generally achieve this dream by simply finding an 8:30 a.m. - 4:30 p.m. job. But to truly be successful, our dreams must go beyond having the ability to pay bills. African immigrants must dream of surviving beyond the pay cheque. This ability will most likely come by exploring talents and discovering unique abilities that African immigrants bring to Canada and exploiting opportunities that lead to success.

Years ago, I read about the famous American dream. In simple words, it simply means in America you have the freedom to be whatever you want to be. To many Americans, this simply means you have the freedom to legally do whatever you wish that will allow you to make as much millions of dollars as you have the ability to.

It's no wonder that in America individuals make millions in a day, over a weekend, or over a year or several years. Ironically, age is not even a major factor. In as much as many of these individuals are sports stars, musicians, filmmakers, many others are not. Instead they are stock traders, entrepreneurs, writers, etc. Individuals dream to own estates, airplanes, and chains of moneymaking systems. You would think that after someone makes a million dollars, they would stop pursuing their dreams, but they never. Day in and day out the same people continue pushing on to expand the fulfillment of their dreams. Isn't this a lesson for African immigrants in Canada, and especially in Manitoba?

Shall African-Canadian immigrants learn a lesson? Yes, just one lesson. It's easy to dispel the pursuit of excellency through wealth as sheer selfishness. But remember, the American dream is not meant to leave anybody behind. It's meant to allow everybody to be involved in the race. True of every race is that there is the one who comes first and the one who comes last. But as long as you have participated in the race, there is a reward for you. You may not get the first prize, but everyone will know that you did your best and you will reap the benefits accordingly.

I also recall when the late President John F. Kennedy of the US once told his nation, "Don't ask what America will do for you, instead ask 'What can I do for America?'" Thinking about these words reminds me of the dreams of African-Canadian immigrants. If as African-Canadians we continue to ask, what will Canada do for us, we may not see any fulfillment of our dreams. However, if we realize that Canada has given us peace and the opportunity and freedom to pursue our dreams, and if we actually focus on pursuing our dreams, we shall turn peace and opportunity into prosperity and power. And that's desirable and acceptable.

Pursuing dreams, of course, will require that we are properly educated. But beyond education, we must exploit our talents to create wealth and wealth making systems. As a way to help shape the future of the sons and daughters of African-Canadians, many parents have taken the initiative to involve their children in extracurricular activities such as music lessons, acting lessons, athletics, football and whatever will help children excel and prosper. Remember to use the magic formula— homework first then extra curricular activities. Using this formula will allow the children of Africans to receive good education and at the same time develop their talents in extracurricular activities.

When I shared the thoughts on this article with one of the African Community leaders, Reg Ejeckam, he made one special observation. Reg observed that we Africans are too cautious and do not want to take any risks with the little money that we have saved to start a business or venture into some unknown with some calculated risk. We have not taken up the opportunities there are to generate more wealth than just salary. "Sometimes I see Africans working tirelessly hard like someone preparing for an examination without an outline or the benefit of past exams. Whereas, if they managed to find some outline then that energy and effort could be more focused and directed where it would yield better results without too much waste," observed Ejeckam.

To wrap up, if every African-Canadian immigrant in Manitoba ventures to do their best at pursuing their dream, I am sure there will be a pack that will be so successful and will bring the African community pride and prosperity. Sure the African community has the potential to prosper. The secret is having a vision and focusing our effort and energy where it would yield better results. Everyone must determine a trade for himself or herself, and pursue it. It's never too late to upgrade skills that will lead us to success. Pursue your dream. Whether it's your career, business, sportsmanship, acting, singing or dancing, whatever you wish to be, pursue. TwCN.

# A Mandate To Complete The War, Hopefully!

I t's George W. Bush again for another four years. Most analysts agree that Bush's re-election is not for the need for him to do anything different from what he has done so far. Rather it is a reaffirmation of the mandate to complete the war in Iraq. Most Americans feel insecure to transfer the responsibility of finishing the mission in Iraq to another leader. Given how tight the race for the white house was, if it were not for the war the Democrats would have had the opportunity to assume the White House. But it will be another four years before they can do so.

Now that Bush is in the White House, what is the implication for Overseas Africans and Africa in general? Generally speaking the majority of African Americans favour the liberal democrats over the conservative republicans. When I hear the terms liberal and conservative, I always ask, "What is it that makes for liberalism or conservatism?"

On one hand, history shows that it was liberalism that brought African Americans such freedom as the freedom from slavery, freedom to vote and freedom to run for political office. It was liberalism that recognized the rights of women to vote and to run for political office and even to drive.

On the other hand history shows that conservatism limited freedoms including fight for continued slavery and fight for restricted voting rights, etc. You see, conservatism, for the most part resists change. Without change continents such as Africa may not have had the opportunity to see independence from colonialism or apartheid. It is

205

such history that makes the majority of African Americans more pro democrat than republican, because it's such change as brought about by liberalism that has benefited African Americans in the past. As for issues pertaining to Overseas Africans in America and Africans on the motherland, it is likely that it will be another four years before rays of hope from the famous White House can reach them.

It is important to recognize the fact that there those Overseas Africans who are liberal and there are those who are conservative. Yes, when in Africa it might be of some benefit to be conservative. Case in point, Mugabe's stand against public tolerance of homosexuality in Zimbabwe. But when you are in the diaspora, conservative Africans may find themselves changing camps and becoming liberal Overseas Africans. For in the diaspora it is often the liberals that embrace values of inclusiveness and tolerance to the benefit of Overseas Africans. For this reason you can't help it but to compromise on some distasteful social issues, and these differ from one person to another.

The reason why Bush may have some African American support is because his conservatism is rooted in his religious life. His stand on social issues, particularly homosexuality and abortion, gained him considerable support that actually made a difference between leaving and remaining in the White House. And in this case, he remains in the White House. So let us be gentlemen and ladies and exercise our democratic right and congratulate him on his win and wish him the very best of his second term as President of the United States of America.

Of much interest is Illinoi's Barack Obama election to the United States Senate. Obama is a forty-two year old African American born to a Kenyan father and American mother. He is a Havard Law School graduate devoted to advancing civil liberties affecting African Americans. He is also a staunch democrat whose race was almost uncontested when his republican rival gave up the race in the Spring. The republicans found a replacement but rather too late.

After his election Obama was asked by CNN what he would advise the president. He said that his advice would be the same to anyone who ends up in the White House. And his advice is to the White House reach out to all democrats and republicans for the purpose of fighting the common enemy. For Americans the common enemy is lack of medical insurance for many African Americans, expensive medical drugs, uncertain social security for seniors, and unemployment. This is not bad advice from a rookie politician heading to the United States Senate.

All in all, of much relevance is the idea of reaching out or building bridges, which is quite critical for all. More so for Overseas Africans who have so many dreams about their lives in the diaspora and the lives of their beloved ones at home. For Overseas Africans, building bridges must include staying united and building stronger communities abroad and, building strong families and consolidating relationships. Where possible, building bridges may include building networks across cities, countries and even continents. And in this process everyone has a role to play either at family level, community level, national or international level. What role are you going to play? TwCN.

---

### An Excerpt from Obama's Speech

*"We will be measured by whether those men all across the state in Galesburg, in Rockford and Decatur and Alton, those folks who have been laid off their jobs, seen their jobs move to Mexico or China, lost their health care, their pensions threatened, whether they are able to find jobs that allow them to support a family and maintain their dignity. We are going to be measured by how well we deliver the resources to the school districts all across the state who are in deficit spending. To make sure that our children have the teachers and the programs they need to excel. We are going to be measured by whether or not we can provide access and affordability to healthcare so that no families in Illinois are bankrupt when they get sick. We are going to be measured by whether our senior citizens can retire with some dignity and some respect. We are going to be measured by the degree to which we can craft a foreign policy in which we are not simply feared in the world but we are also respected. That's what we are going to be measured by."* - **Barack Obama**, November 2, 2004 Obama's Election Victory Speech.

---

# Why You Should Hire Me, a Visible Minority

The "Voice of Visible Minorities Speaking Out on Breaking Down Barriers," published by the Conference Board of Canada (September 2004) is a very interesting reading. The briefing touches on many barriers to success experienced by visible minority professionals and that we at TwCN have shared before. We would encourage all Overseas Africans to read this briefing and keep a copy for future reference.

Of interest, however, is the briefing's point on page 4 that:

*". . . the source of pressure was co-workers' suspicions that jobs or promotions went to people because they were visible minorities, not because they had the appropriate competencies and skills."*

How do you respond to this pressure? TwCN recognizes some myth in this statement. And we will try to remove that myth.

First, be it known that if you are a visible minority, it is because of your competencies and skills that you set foot into your employer's workplace. One way to look at it is that once you have gainful employment, being a visible minority should no longer be a liability but an asset.

Secondly, if indeed you are promoted based on the fact that you are a visible minority; it is only because your employer has recognized you as an asset. In other words, you bring more to the workplace than just competencies and skills that the average of the visible majority has. You make your employer look great in the eyes of customers or the marketplace. In other words, you bring diversity to the workplace which is an asset in today's competitive national and/or global economy.

Whether public or private, employers usually have other goals in addition to getting skilled and competent employees. Some of these goals include increased diversity to reflect the diversity of customers and expansion into new markets. "I would like you to hire me because of my skills and not because I am a visible minority," is a preferred response for most minorities who need to be hired or promoted. I for one would like to say "I would like you to hire me, yes because of my skills and competencies, but also because I am a visible minority." And I will tell you why?

Often, it is people who believe they are qualified for an advertised or available vacancy that apply for the position. It therefore, appears that appropriate qualifications are the common denominator. If all who are interviewed do well on the interview, then some other criterion must be used for hiring. And that criterion must contribute to meeting the other objectives of the employer. If diversity is one such other objective, then let it be; and as a visible minority let me help my employer meet that other objective.

Hard to accept, for some people, is the color or ethnicity criterion. Indeed if one of the corporate goals is to increase diversity in the workplace, then I should be hired based first on my skills and competencies and secondly on the fact that I am a visible minority.

Again, don't misunderstand the issue here, the primary criteria is appropriate qualifications, the secondary criteria must help to meet other objectives even if it happens to be the color or ethnicity criteria. So both criteria must be accepted as appropriate when it comes to hiring or promoting visible minorities. It is a fact of life and we all must come to terms with it and admit it as such.

Being a visible minority should, however, be an issue if you are not qualified. And if you are not qualified then you should not even be in the picture in the first place.

So, next time you are challenged with co-workers' suspicions that you are hired or promoted because you are a visible minority, simply tell them that you are an asset; you bring more to the workplace than they do; you make the workplace a better place for all and the management team recognizes that fact and is proud of it. TwCN.

# ACCHC Project - Expectations and Reality

The initiative by the African Community in Manitoba, Canada, to build the African Canadian Cultural and Heritage Centre (ACCHC) in Winnipeg has been described by some as a "very ambitious project." At TwCN we can't help but ask, "Is the ACCHC project really very ambitious?" And in keeping with our mission, we thought we could use this edition of TwCN and try to address both expectations and reality about the project. By so doing, we hope we will put the project in perspective, especially for community members and others concerned, to understand.

*Expectations*

Generally speaking, one would say that the African community expected to simply do their part and inform the three levels of government. And the three levels of government would simply do their part and write cheques.

In other words, the African community expected to prepare a business plan, submit it to the three levels of government, and other potential funders, and promptly receive promises of funds or even see cheques written to finance the project. Also members of the community perhaps expect to hear that the land has been offered, we have the money, and the contractor to start building the facility.

This indeed is good for expectations. However, the reality is different.

## The Reality

Only experience reveals reality about any project. This is true for the ACCHC project as well. And no one knows this better than the Chair himself and his supportive committee of African community leaders. Reality shows that it is not that simple. There are processes or a system of doing things especially when a project involves millions of dollars. Simply put the system involves processes including community mobilization for the project, networking with potential funders, identifying sponsors, conducting a feasibility study for the project, planning and designing the project, construction of the centre, turnover and start up of centre operations.

## Mobilizing the community

Community mobilization is a grassroots level task. This is where every community member is required to respond to the call to support the project. This is where every community leader is required to demonstrate their leadership and lead by uniting their community members behind the project.

Community mobilization is critical because project sponsors are looking for this support to ensure that there are no divisions within the African community about the project. Unity of purpose and of action at community level is one of the critical keys to the success of the project. No wonder the African Community Secretariat is committed to advancing community unity and prosperity. And it appears in all respects that the ACCHC project is larger than any particular individual or group and deserves everyone's support.

## Networking with potential funders

Everyone wishes it were as simple as simply preparing a business plan and submitting it with a request for funding, and being able to get cheques written. Unfortunately, it's not that simple. Leaders and champions of the ACCHC project must establish rapport and gain the confidence of funders and sponsors. This rapport and confidence is not achieved without investing time and effort in meeting with potential funders and sponsors. It is therefore, important for community members to support their leaders in their effort to meet with other community leaders, professionals, business executives, and politicians for purposes of strengthening relationships and gaining their confidence.

During networking meetings there are no commitments made. Yes, you may hear about recommendations, references, and suggestions, but there are no binding decisions or contracts signed. Binding decisions and contracts have their place later in the system. It is in the networking process that our community leaders must demonstrate that they are competent to handle the project and that they are accountable to their community and to all stakeholders including funders and sponsors.

Networking also should help to increase the credibility of the project. If some heavyweights within the Winnipeg community are brought on board in support of the project, the project will have more credibility, which will be an asset in convincing more sponsors to support the project.

If networking works and credibility is built for the project, then sponsors will eagerly provide financial support while being convinced that they know who they are writing the cheques to, and confident that the financial resources will be managed and used responsibly.

*Identifying sponsors*

Sponsors are organizations, that is government or private, and individuals who actually provide financial resources for the project. For the ACCHC project, sponsors may include the African community organizations and individuals, the three levels of government, selected foundations, international and nationally renowned individuals, and others. Identifying these sponsors need not be the work of the Chair alone. The whole community must be involved. Moreover, there is need to establish a way to encourage sponsors to come forth, and a way to remember their contribution to the ACCHC.

*Conducting a feasibility study for the project*

Generally, projects that involve public funding or borrowing of financial resources always require a feasibility study. A feasibility study makes for Stage I of the project and includes project formulation and strategy design and approval.

The feasibility study forms the basis for one significant decision: GO or NO-GO decision. Thus far, no feasibility study has been done for the ACCHC project. Since the ACCHC project involves millions of dollars a feasibility study is a must. Given that some potential funders have described the ACCHC project as "very ambitious" the feasibility study will provide well grounded justification for the ACCHC business plan. In other words, the feasibility study will show how the business plan is, in fact, doable.

The question that the African community should be asking and hopefully find an answer to is, "Who will do this feasibility study?" It must be someone who has the interest of the African community at heart. And even more important is the question, "Does the African community have the knowledge, skills and expertise to conduct their own feasibility study or to work in partnership with other experts? Are these skills, knowledge and expertise well packaged? Are they actively being employed or will they simply be resumed when the request comes?" Whoever is involved, there is need to be objective and to demonstrate capability and possibly past accomplishments.

Since the feasibility study involves employing a professional, it has the potential to consume financial resources. For the ACCHC project, the African community must find some "seed money" to finance the feasibility study.

Once the feasibility study has been conducted and the decision is a GO decision, then this decision becomes a reference point for all fundraising efforts. At this point even stakeholders who otherwise would be reluctant to finance the project may be awakened and approached for financial support.

*Planning and designing the project*

If the feasibility study results in a GO decision for the project, then Stage II of the project must begin. This stage involves official planning and design of the project and includes base design, cost and schedule, contract terms and conditions, and detailed planning. For the ACCHC project this stage is in not too far a distant future.

But whether or not we get into it will depend on the results of the feasibility study. In the meantime, networking must continue.

*Construction of the centre*

The construction phase comprises Stage III of the ACCHC project. Assuming that land is allocated, after successful planning and design, and if there are enough funds raised, then construction of the ACCHC will begin. Custom materials will be manufactured and delivered, civil works will be done, fixtures will be installed and landscaping will be completed.

During the construction phase, Africans can drive by the site and confidently say, "That is the African centre coming up. We will be celebrating our culture and teaching our children in that centre. We will meet with other Canadians in that Centre." At the end of the construction phase the ACCHC facility will be complete.

*Turnover and start up of centre operations*

Just before turnover and start-up or Stage IV, the ACCHC facility will be tested to ensure that everything is in good working condition. To ensure that systems like lighting, sewer, water, emergency, and heating are all in excellent condition the city of Winnipeg will conduct comprehensive tests before the occupancy permit is issued. Once the occupancy permit is issued, then the Board of Directors will be handed the keys to the centre.

I can imagine the Board, as their first order of business in the new facility, making a press release thanking all stakeholders including the builders, sponsors and the Winnipeg community for helping turn a long dream into reality and announcing the official opening date.

*The task ahead and conclusion*

When the facility becomes operational at the end of the construction stage, the ACCHC Business Plan and, most importantly, the Constitution will then become more relevant and will need to be implemented. Before this happens, finding generous supporters and willing sponsors and winning their confidence is the major task ahead of the African community initiative.

At any rate, the African community must not be discouraged in anyway. Rather, the community should work within the reality framework. By following all the necessary steps of the system, as on an automobile assembly line, the ACCHC dream will be achieved. In the event of facing hurdles and obstacles, community members and our leaders should constantly look for innovative ways to jump hurdles and creative ways to go around obstacles. TwCN.

# One Big Secret for Overseas African Business Success

T he desire to be economically and financially independent is one main reason for going through school and college, and finding work or starting a business. Growing up in Africa, I used to see people spend day in and day out selling merchandize at the market. By arrangement people selling the same product such as fish, beans or vegetables occupied the same area at the market. When I was sent to go fetch something like beans or fish, I often got confused because I didn't just know from whom to buy what I needed. But I took my time. I started by walking through the aisle closely observing every heap of beans or fish. I was, however, confused when it was so difficult to tell the difference between the products. In my eyes as a young person, they all looked the same.

In order to decide from whom to buy, I had to use a different criterion. I looked at the people selling the good. I considered how presentable they were. I remember being attracted to buy from those that wore appropriate attire and looked most presentable.

I also remember there were those sellers who actually shouted at me "pano ba kastoma" meaning "here customer." They did this in order to attract not only my attention, but also the attention of other shoppers. And those with sweet soprano voices often attracted my attention, and many times I ended up buying from them. As I think about this experience, one question that comes to mind now is "Why should anybody under the sun bother telling a story of his shopping experience as a young lad in Africa?"

*Much Needed Critical Support*

Well, there must be a good reason. Overseas Africans are increasingly becoming entrepreneurial. This is particularly evidenced by overseas Africans in Winnipeg, Manitoba, Canada, where TwCN is based. A good number of them have started or are planning to start businesses. As expected, these entrepreneurs are deservedly vying for support from the overseas African community as well as the larger community.

I would like to believe that overseas Africans everywhere are eager to support overseas African businesses. However, I am afraid to say that I don't think overseas Africans want to provide support at the expense of better customer service. Perhaps if you are an overseas African who owns a business you might be asking, "What do you mean by better customer service? Is it not good enough that I have a business and I am a boss?" Hmmm! Please allow me opportunity to share what common sense shows overseas African shoppers are looking for in overseas African owned businesses.

In Africa, if you are a millionaire entrepreneur, it's like you are untouchable. You can do anything under the sun, and the path to your business will still be congested with passionate customers. And the reason is, in many places particularly small towns and villages people hardly have any choices. Often they have only one place from which to buy salt, cooking oil or shoes. It's not like overseas in North America or Europe and elsewhere where people have a choice. And because people overseas have a choice, business owners do everything in their power to attract and retain valued customers.

*Better Customer Service, the One Big Secret*

Here is a sample of some things you can do to provide better customer service and attract and retain overseas Africans to support your business:

1. **Accessibility** – ensure that your business is accessible by both physically fit and challenged customers.

2. **Accuracy** – provide accurate change or information all the time or fill your customer orders accurately.

3.  **Attentiveness/Helpfulness** – pay attention to the needs of your customers and offer to provide a solution if you can.

4.  **Availability** – make yourself available when customers need you.

5.  **Care** – demonstrate care for your customers when they are doing business with you.

6.  **Clarity** – make your communications or directions clear for your customers to easily understand and/or know.

7.  **Cleanliness/Tidiness** – make every aspect of your business premises clean and tidy. This includes the appearance of your staff on duty; ensure they are presentable. If your business involves handling food, leave no doubts about hygiene in the minds of your customers.

8.  **Comfort** – make your premises comfortable and when you speak to your customers help them feel comfortable.

9.  **Commitment** – commit yourself to doing everything in your power to satisfy your customers.

10. **Communication** – invite your customers whenever you can. Communicate with your customers any problems you might have in delivering your services or products. Customers will understand and appreciate your frankness.

11. **Competence** – ensure that your team of staff or employees is competent to provide services in a professional manner. If your employees need improved competence consider training them.

12. **Completeness** – make sure that you fill your customer orders completely or if they need information make sure it is complete.

13. **Consistence** – provide services to all your customers in the same way day in and day out. And choose the very best way to provide services.

14. **Convenience** – serve your customers using a place and time most convenient to your customers.

15. **Courtesy** – always remember to be courteous to your customers. It's part of being professional.

16. **Ease of use** – if you have equipment or facility that customers have to use, make sure it is easy to use.

17. **Fitness for use** – similar to ease of use, if you have equipment or facility that customers have to use make sure it is fit for use.

18. **Flexibility** – customers come in various sizes and shapes and for different reasons, be flexible to accommodate them all.

19. **Friendliness** – a smile on your face and a friendly chart will help show that you are friendly and customers who perceive you as a friend will always come back.

20. **Integrity** – It's very much personal, but keeping your promises with customers will engender trust and confidence in you and your business, and they will always come back, or speak about you and your business to others.

21. **Perceived value** – customers will always ask, is it really worthy it doing business with you? It's all about perception, so do your best to positively influence their perception.

22. **Quantity** – what ever you are providing, do you have enough resources to meet demand. You don't want your customers to experience shortages.

23. **Reliability** – can your customers count on you all the time? How reliable are you? It's part of integrity.

24. **Responsiveness** – business flourishes when services or products are provided in response to the needs of customers. If your customer has a need respond with a solution.

25. **Security** – overseas Africans leave Africa for many reasons and one reason is insecurity. Make your customers feel secure on your premises and in doing business with you.

26. **Time/Timeliness** – Tell your customers the time you are available to serve them and make sure you serve them at that time.

*Customer Focus, the Ultimate Key*

In the land of abundance like Canada, the USA and the UK, where overseas African businesses are mushrooming, customers often have a choice. And often the customer service experience is a key factor in making that choice. Like the lifeblood of any business is in sales, so is the lifeblood of overseas African businesses. And in the face of competing resources, a prudent entrepreneur will make customer service the least of reasons to kill his or her business. In other words, if nothing helps to build your business, let customer service do.

At the market in Africa, when the beans or the fish or vegetables looked all the same, I often decided to buy from the seller who communicated with me well or most, or who pleased me by being neat and presentable. "Pano ba kastoma" was a call demonstrating desire to meet the needs of the customer and to draw the customer's attention. I can't forget how those marketers focused on me as their customer.

Today, I see the opportunity for overseas African business owners to develop their businesses by focusing on their customers and squarely meeting their needs. TwCN.

# Celebrate the African Spirit

D ecember is one significant month for many families. It is well known for bringing in the Christmas season. But Christmas means many different things to many different people. To those who believe in Christ, it means celebrating Christ's birth. To those who are in business it means consumerism. Yet to others it means time for exchanging gifts.

True, some overseas Africans share these meanings of Christmas. And to many the month of December and the Christmas season mean peace, joy, love and goodwill. Actually, it means taking advantage and taking the opportunity to mend burnt bridges, share love and joy and extend the spirit of goodwill to others.

Overseas Africans come from diverse backgrounds in Africa. Some parts of Africa have known nothing but peace and tranquility, but these are very few. Most areas in Africa have known war and crime. One wonders whether a season such as Christmas season means anything to certain parts of Africa. Perhaps its time for overseas Africans living in the peaceful and tranquil west to remind their homefolks to seek peace and joy, and exercise love and goodwill towards other people including their supposed enemies.

It is unfortunate that Africa is known abroad mostly for its wars, droughts, poverty and civil unrests. These experiences, unfortunately, cover-up the beauty of Africa which is not founded in material things, but in the sunshine and goodwill of its people. Africans shine and it shows. Africans, generally have and share a joyous spirit. As a matter of fact, this reminds me of a comment that one of my colleagues always makes. He sincerely believes that Africans are generally happy people. They are always smiling. Thinking about it more, I find my friend's comment to be very revealing. The smiles of Africans reveal the wonderful spirit of Africa. As Dr. Zephania Matanga observes, "Africans don't take time to celebrate the African spirit, the good in Africans."

At TwCN, we wish to take the opportunity to remind overseas Africans to celebrate the African spirit of joy, love, peace and goodwill. Yes, these attributes of Christmas may have been denied most Africans because of wars and poverty, but they should not be forgotten. In the land of tranquility as overseas Africans experience abroad, Africans need to come together and celebrate the African spirit, including reminding one another that we are a great and strong people. We may have been driven out of our countries, we may have suffered hunger as a result of drought, we may have given up on our leaders, but we are a great and strong people. This is strongly evidenced by the fact that our smiles are wide, our voices are deep, our thoughts are inspiring and our hearts are warm.

Yes, there are those overseas Africans who never succeed at shedding negative attitudes towards their fellow Africans. But these carry an unnecessary burden on their hearts. They are always despising others seeking to see perfection in imperfection. Yet the truth is there is as much imperfection in anyone of us as anyone of us would want to see.

Lastly, note that it's Christmas time. Please take advantage, take the opportunity and mend fences, build bridges by extending a hand of love, a mouth of joy, a heart of goodwill to your family, fellow overseas Africans and all others during this season. Enjoy the month, enjoy the season. From your team at TwCN accept our love, joy, peace and goodwill. TwCN.

# Unity: the Master Key to Achieving the African Centre in Manitoba

How united is the African community on this project? is a frequent question many a people who are coming across the African Canadian Cultural and Heritage Centre (ACCHC) business plan are asking. The question, of course, is genuine. And the African community in Manitoba has to live and demonstrate that it is a united community on this project. The African Communities of Manitoba, Inc. (ACOMI) is the uniting umbrella organization. As of now, ACOMI can boast of being at its best, but realizes it is just at the beginning of continual improvement in running its community affairs.

ACOMI is steered by a committee of leaders of various African community organizations and individuals who may not belong to any organization because they have no critical mass. Like the Africa Pavilion is a child of ACOMI, so is the ACCHC. But the ACCHC will be the future home of the Africa Pavilion.

*What has the potential to divide the Manitoba African community?*

Country of origin, English or French language, tribe, political experience, and community leaders have the potential to divide the African community. Associations based on countries are good, but do have their own disadvantages. Unless the leaders are engaged and interested in uniting their country based community with the rest of the community, members may praise only their group and despise the rest of the community. The truth is country based organizations are for administrative convenience only and are not an end in themselves.

English or French speaking people find it easy to associate together. Again, unless Africans realize the need to stay united despite of language differences, English or French can be a barrier to unity. Canada is a bilingual country and English and French have the right to be used simultaneously and interchangeably. English and French should not be an issue in having Africans united on the ACCHC initiative.

Africans come from different tribes. Some tribes are known for their domineering attitudes towards other tribes. But hopefully while in Canada, tribe does not matter. As a matter of fact, being in Canada should provide us opportunity to see how ridiculous it is to be tribal. Instead, our common experiences must pull us together.

Also, political experiences are a reason for many Africans to come to Canada as refugees. Those who hold dear their political affiliations may continue to work here raising money and sending it back to Africa to support their political masters. Somewhat true also is that some Africans may be reluctant to join with others because the bigger group includes some people who are politically affiliated. This may as well be unfortunate. Hopefully people who remain affiliated with politics in Africa will come to their senses and cease such affiliation. Everyone's genuine desire should be being part of the united African-Canadians.

*Community vision and goal*

The vision of every African-Canadian should be to make the African community, a community of choice for the future generation of African-Canadians. Indeed, the motivation and the passion of the people steering the ACCHC lies in their vision to build a community of African-Canadians. A future generation that will be born and grow in peace. This generation knows no African country boundary. Africa to this generation appears to be one big country like Canada.

What then, must be the goal for every African-Canadian? Every African-Canadian should identify the source of division and work hard to overcome that source of division. The common experiences as Africans re: daily challenges to make our ends meet, daily challenges to upgrade our education, daily challenges to get employed, and daily challenges to attend to our children and fulfill their interests while protecting them against destructive habits, must bring us together and keep us united. As a united front African Canadians will overcome these challenges and make the future of their children better than the present.

*The key role of African community leaders*

African community leaders have such an important role that perhaps they don't realize they do. Every community leader has a solemn responsibility of educating its community and rallying them behind every community initiative. And today, the major initiative is the development of the ACCHC, as a home for the Manitoba African community of the future. As a master key opens every door in a building, so will African community unity make possible the achievement of the ACCHC dream. All African Community leaders must be part of this initiative and rally their members behind it. If the community stays united in building it, it will stay united in using it.

Individual Africans should also have special interest in knowing what's going on in their community, and in particular, with the ACCHC. Ask your leaders and help them serve you better. As your leaders, they have the power that obligates them to lead you in the right direction, for the right purpose, toward the right goal and for the right reasons. And the ACCHC is a right direction, purpose, goal and reason.

*It's Christmas time and what's your gift to your community*

Lastly, those who celebrate the Christmas season, and most Africans do, know that Christmas is about love, peace, joy and goodwill. But more importantly, Christmas is also about gifts. A gift is something you receive unexpectedly and undeservedly. It's a surprise. Would you have a surprise for the ACCHC this Christmas season? You can give unity, you can give funds, and you can give your support. TwCN.

## HONORING THE READERS

# TwCN Celebrates One Year of Achievement - Part 1

I t was once a vision, a day in the future. But now it's right here. That's the day Dr. Ntungo writes and publishes the 52$^{nd}$ TwCN article. And it's worth celebrating. Mmmm! I have to munch some chocolates. After all, it's Christmas season.

How would you spend your anniversary date? It's only appropriate to look back and reflect on the remarkable achievement and the people that made it happen. Once you do that then you could sit down and develop another vision for the near future. As once promised, the 52$^{nd}$ edition of TwCN is dedicated to readers and the people who take the time to provide feedback and encouragement to the Editorial Director and Publisher. Without you, we would not have the inspiration and motivation to produce one remarkable TwCN after another.

Now here are some of the selected feedback and comments that, at least in principle, deserve a TwCN award.

*Observations from Home*

"Thanks once again. A few observations and comments: South Africa has finally emerged as a big powerful impetus to African Development. What you have observed in Zambia is true of Uganda, Kenya and lots of other African Countries. They captured the Cell phone explosion perfectly through MTN. They are in Supermarkets and Malls as well as textiles.

However we the indigenous people can still exploit a few arbitrage situations like the price of calling cards. I am discouraged to learn that the government allows people to use the US$ as a currency. The best way would be for the government to allow entrepreneurs to set up foreign exchange bureaus regulated by the Zambian Central Bank as to exchange rates bands. That way it is encouraging entrepreneurship and also creating another source of licensing and various tax revenues.[1]

It is also sad about the neglect of the essential services that have to be financed as a community. In this case the government acts as a conduit by collecting money from the people through the tax system and then using that money to provide the following essential services:

1. Air Traffic Control
2. Highway Construction and Maintenance
3. Provincial and municipal road and rubbish collection
4. Military Defense. This seems to be the only service that gets most of the attention. The more corrupt the Government the higher the military spending. OOH! I wonder why?
5. Civic Policing
6. Education
7. Health Care
8. Civil Service (or more appropriately the corruption, patronage and wastage service in most of our African nations)

So you are quite right in your observation that somebody is not doing their job and also misusing the communal funds collected through taxation." - *Jim Kasule* on TwCN No. 7.

*Zambian Leadership Challenged*

"Thank you Ntungo for using Zambia to highlight problems that are common to the whole of Mother Africa. Before I give my thoughts, I have to point out that you have always to strive for political correctness, therefore use a neutral pronoun to donate a country or use both him and her when you are referring to a country.

---

[1] Note that US$ was used after being converted from the local currency Kwacha. Zambia does not use US$ for domestic transactions.

You are being kind to The Zambian President by describing his ill informed utterances as temporary insanity. They are downright stupid.

Challenge the Zambian ministry of Finance to tabulate Foreign Direct Investments (FDI) that are contributed by Zambians in the Diaspora. Be it to relatives, Health, Education or just plain business investments. Evaluate the top-notch professional advice that flows freely from Zambians in the Diaspora into Zambia in a milliard of ways. When the Government of Uganda (to their credit) undertook such a study, the figures were eye openers to the Government. Ugandans in the Diaspora are the top foreign exchange earners to the country. Edging out the traditional cash earners (Coffee, Cotton, Sugar, and Copper including tourism). Further more this type of FDI is always increasing from year to year as more and more of us realize that we are the only social security provider for our relatives back home. Better still there are no ties attached to such FDI except that the businesses started have to be self sustaining (Remember that free advice).

As a Zambian living in the Diaspora, you do not need to be ashamed of yourself. The only way you should feel ashamed is if you have forgotten your past. "If you don't know your past, you don't know your future" — Ziggy Marley. If you are a positive contributing member of the society/country of your choice be it as a student, an employee, an employer, or a professional academic; please do hold your head high. You are one of the best ambassadors (without pay) for Zambia and Africa in general.

The path of countries moving very rapidly on the development ladder is directly proportional on how such countries treat their members in the Diaspora.

All of you know the story of India, as the Patels' go back home with their attained brain power, Bill Gates, All major US companies, The Generals (Equipment, Motors etc) are not far behind setting up virtual offices and call centers in India to service the American Public. Talk about a jobless US economic recovery!! This trend is happening in China, Singapore, South Africa, Korea, Taiwan, Mexico, Israel, Pakistan, Vietnam. The list of countries that are taking advantage of their educated ambassadors is growing by leaps and bounds. Why is Africa always the last to wake up on such cheap positive trends?

Africa has to recognize its brainpower and allow dual citizenship in order to encourage meaningful economic participation by its Diaspora workforce. Wake up Zambia! Wake up Africa!!" - *Jim Kasule* on TwCN No. 8.

"I read your article entitled *'When Leading Zambia Becomes Tough, Guard Against Leadership Frustration.'*

It made very interesting reading and as a Zambian I agreed and equally sympathized with all other Zambians living abroad. The first time I listened to the President talk about this issue, I did not agree with him and I was so affected as though I was the one living abroad.

I have a few friends abroad and I know how much they send every so often to support families back here in Zambia. I am sure the government should be totally appreciative of this fact. Surely, somebody is taking care of those of Zambia's citizens who the government cannot take care of and whether the Zambians abroad are talking more than the government can bare then it is only that they are reacting because they are meant to bare that which the government cannot.

It is a fact that we are poor and the politics are also not right. Advice on what can help us to come out of this misery should come from every Zambian who really understands our miseries whether within the country or outside. The fact that we do listen to non-Zambians who sometimes dictate their 'advice' then we should be ready to listen to those of our brothers who may be better informed than ourselves out there. For example the president traveled to India and China to learn on how these people manage to feed themselves, surely he could have used Zambians who live in these countries to tell him exactly how the people in these countries manage to feed themselves despite their huge population.

You are in fact our ambassadors. The president needs to instead sit with you people and ask you to send even more help to Zambia here at home so that he can be relieved of the pressures which make him not enjoy the presidency.

Surely it is time we stopped insulting each other and started listening to each other. It is the only way we are going to see ourselves out of the mess we have gotten ourselves into. Long Live Zambia." - *Robert Nguni* on TwCN No. 8.

"Hello Editor, I sometimes receive articles by Ntungo from a colleague via email. I would like to be receiving from you if possible various articles by your organization. Regards." - *Willis Muhanga* on TwCN No. 8.

*Outcry Left to Others*

"Thank you for raising our awareness as usual. As Africans living away from the varieties of miseries that beseech our continent from time to time, we have become so numb that we leave the outcry to others. Perhaps, it is time those of us in Winnipeg organize biannual rallies to highlight the plights of Africa. God knows that we are not short of issues that continue to plaque our continent. It is amazing what Winnipeggers can do to influence the politics of the moment!!!! Have a nice weekend." - *Bose Agbayewa* on TwCN No. 28.

*American Election*

"Just some correction I thought the American election is on November 2nd. I could be wrong!!!" - *Charter M. Kidzugane* on TwCN No. 43.

"You are dead right the American elections will be held on November 2nd. Let me also take this opportunity to thank Ntungo for a well documented article and for bringing awareness to our community on matters of such importance. No doubt Africa still has a great mountain to climb when it comes to democratic tenets, rights and freedoms of her sons and daughters. However we should not forget the mere fact that there was a time in our history when African presidents used to stand for elections alone with no challenger at all in those mockery elections of the past years. The party and its government theory was so strong that it was seen as taboo to challenge the incumbent president, if anything you risked your life if you did try.

Today, the landscape in some African countries is slowly changing, despite resistance to change in the form of election ringing suppression of opposition voices, killing of civil and human rights activist and indeed opposition leaders, Africans have risen to the occasion in form of Trade Unions, NGOs, opposition parties and are now challenging governments.

We have seen some countries change their constitutions in order to remove some impediments that disadvantage the masses; we have seen changes such as that which restricts a president to reign for only two terms. The so called dark continent is slowly but surely waking up, her sons and daughters are prepared to ensure that the great continent fully stands up they refuse to be curled into surrender some have already paid the ultimate price sacrificing with their own blood while others still continue to sacrifice. I have come to believe that freedom does not come on a silver plate. There is always sacrifice, Christians will tell you Jesus sacrificed to free humanity, Moslems like wise they will tell you Mohammed sacrificed to free humanity and many other religions of the world will subscribe to the same line of thought.

Today, we admire the United States of America because their forefathers sacrificed in order for them to attain the freedoms and the values that they now enjoy. I have said it before and I will say it again, for Africa to be near or reach the standards that we are talking about, her sons and daughters will have to be optimistic about tomorrow, certainly the atrocities of yesterday and today should not dim the prosperity that comes with tomorrow. We all must find a way to contribute to the well-being of Africa. It does not matter where we are, we must try if we can to contribute in whatever form we can, either economically, politically, civic or in a humanitarian way. And still others are helping Africa through church institutions. Some countries are doing tremendously well when it comes to democratic principles, such as Botswana, Namibia, South Africa, Mozambique Mauritius, et cetera.

Once more my many thanks to Ntungo for so articulate and highly educative an article. May God bless the community." - *Isaac Katoyo* on TwCN No. 43.

## HONORING THE READERS

# TwCN Celebrates One Year of Achievement - Part 2

What a week it has been! Wonderful and encouraging, indeed. Thanks to all who took the time to send in congratulatory messages. Your time and your encouraging messages are appreciated and well received. You will notice that this is Part 2 of TwCN's time to honor the readers and celebrate one year of achievement. So we continue from where we left in TwCN No. 52.

*It's Okay to have Opposing Views*

"Very powerful message, Ntungo! There are lessons for us even within our community here. It is okay to have opposing views. We can debate on issues whether it is to do with Folklorama, the Africa Centre or how we raise our kids and still agree to disagree." – *Hlezi Sy* on TwCN No. 43.

"It's nice to note that some people in our community are talking about the principle of agreeing to disagree. This is a great principle that has helped countries such as Canada, the U.S. and many other western countries to be where they are today. The desire to tolerate each other and/or one another's opposing views yet co-exist is critical to the well-being of any group, community and indeed a nation. And our community is no exception.

The other aspect that is equally important to a community such as ours is self-critic. It is not health for any system to look at criticism as being personal. There is constructive criticism and it can be a very helpful tool for self evaluation. A system that does not evaluate itself risks stagnation or existing in name. I am one admirer of the work that Dr. Ntungo has been doing at the secretariat and if we all give him support a lot can be achieved.

Having said the above, let me now engage the community on some issues that I feel need addressing. Please feel free to correct me where I go wrong, because it's important that the community be well informed. Some time back I brought up the issue of the constitution for the African Community of Manitoba Inc. (ACOMI). A response came which indicated that there was no constitution, and this left me to wonder how the community was operating without anything as a guide.

I further asked how the leadership came into being; suggestions were that it came into existence through a non elective method, whatever that method was. The question that we need to ask ourselves is, "Where does our leadership draw its mandate in the absence of an election?" At this point I am sure you are getting to understand why Ntungo's article is so important and why the United States is so great a country. Legitimacy is imperative for any system to function successfully. But I am not suggesting that in our case only an election can legitimize leadership. However, any other process that is widely acknowledged by the general membership is welcome.

ACOMI is said to be the umbrella organization uniting all other African organizations. Is it, therefore, not a puzzle that country organizations and others such as the African-Canadian Cultural and Heritage Centre, Inc. (ACCHCI), have well tabulated rules, constitutions and also hold elections to legitimize office bearers.

Our community has various organizational groups, they range from NGOs such as African-Canadian Disability Community Association (ACDCA), International African Child Relief and Peace Foundation of Canada (IACRPFC), Sudanese Relief and Rehabilitation Program (SRRP), regional organizations such as the Southern African Association of Manitoba (SAAM), country organizations such as Ghanaian Union, Nigerian Association of Manitoba to name but a few. Then you have youth organizations and finally private businesses. For ACOMI to be a truly umbrella body of the above institutions, we who are members need to come up with a structure at ACOMI that meets the aspirations of these various groups. This is purely the reason why I am in support of Ntungo's initiative of the African-Canadian Community System. I personally believe that there is need for a structure if we are to methodically access say, government departments, a fact that Ntungo alluded to in his article two or so weeks ago.

As a community we have quite a number of highly educated people, very motivated and seriously responsibly holding very good jobs in all levels of government. We also have some in the private sector and NGOs. These are people we could attract and have them get involved with the community; after all they belong to this very community. Sometimes people refrain from community activities because of some people who take every criticism as a personal attack. And those in leadership who do not know how to use words whenever there is a dispute. Those who aspire for leadership they must be responsible people who understand the people on whom they exercise their leadership.

*Ours is a Diverse Community*

Our community is made up of people from different spots of Africa. Some people are coming from hot spots were they have witnessed the most serious atrocities, anything to do with quarrels or infighting or usage of certain words that they considered traumatic will not attract them to the community. They will choose to keep away rather than participate. There are those who are coming from dictatorial territories were people feared even their own shadows; they did not trust the next person, these are generally reserved, they talk less and they choose their words very carefully, and on top of that they are very suspicious. And then you have those who came from the free spots, so to say for the lack of a better word, most of them coming as international students and some on work permits, these are much freer and extremely participatory.

It follows therefore that leadership must understand the make up of our community if they are to attract people to community activities and also if they are to address some of their fears and problems. As for our community membership, please feel free to participate in ACOMI and all other community organizations. Canada conveys on all her people (you included) great rights; rights of free speech, rights of assembly, rights of free movement, et cetera and so you have nothing to fear because the law is there to protect you. God bless you all." - *Isaac Katoyo* on TwCN No. 43.

"Thanks for prompt and good article. I encourage you to attend some of the ACOMI meetings. These issues have been discussed and Dr. KC Prince Asagwara volunteered to table a draft constitution to be reviewed and adopted. My mandate is to facilitate these issues for us to have an election by the end of the year. These salient points were emphasized in my article during this year's Folklorama. It is our collective effort to see which direction ACOMI should take and how best we could run our affairs. Whatever loose structure that was in place helped us set the momentum and moved us so far. Now it is time to legitimize it. Regards." - *Roger Amenyogbe, Acting Chair – ACOMI* on TwCN No. 43.

"Thank you brother chairman for your quick feed back. This indicates a way forward and for sure I am encouraged. God bless." - *Isaac Katoyo* on TwCN No. 43.

"Ba Mudala, this is a great one. It is an eye opener and very informative. I can see that God led my feet to get to know Chrispin." – *Delphin Mutaka* on TwCN No. 49.

*Looking Forward to the Next 50 TwCNs*

"Ntungo, Congratulations on the 50th episode of TwCN. It is very remarkable. I look forward to reading your articles every Thursday. You've enlightened me on a lot of issues and even the article of your visit to Zambia, as private as it might have been, it is reminiscent of what most of us experience on our visit home. Looking forward to the next 50 TwCNs and more to come. Cheers!" - *Roger Amenyogbe* on TwCN No. 50.

As you can see, with remarkable TwCN articles, it has been a remarkable year indeed. And if TwCN has helped inspire you to act on that important issue, know your community better, go for that dream, then it has fulfilled its mission.

Roger Amenyogbe has set the standard for TwCN in 2005. It's now our goal to develop and publish at least 50 more remarkable TwCNs in 2005. Thank you all for being there and being such ardent readers and contributors to TwCN. May God bless you all most abundantly. TwCN.

# About the Author

Chrispin Ntungo is a self-published author of **Turning Your Dreams into Reality – Personal Planning Guide for Success and Prosperity**, and an African immigrant living in Canada dedicated to enhancing personal and professional development of others. Since 1996, Chrispin Ntungo has served as a part-time advisor on immigration, employment and small business development issues.

After helping hundreds of modern-day immigrants develop strategies for their lives overseas, Chrispin Ntungo founded Thursday with Chrispin Ntungo (TwCN) in 2003. Through TwCN people come and spend Thursday with Chrispin Ntungo. Anyone from the audience can ask Chrispin Ntungo questions related to immigrant experiences, including accomplishments, challenging issues, and dreams. In turn, Chrispin Ntungo provides advice that not only inspires, but also motivates and empowers the listeners and readers. The advice is summarized in form of a story every Thursday highlighting accomplishments, challenges and dreams of immigrants. The popularity of these stories speaks volumes to their practicality and relevance in the lives of modern-day immigrants.

Chrispin Ntungo is well known for his commitment to promoting unity and prosperity amongst immigrants, particularly those from Africa. To help achieve this Chrispin Ntungo established the African Community Secretariat based in Winnipeg, Manitoba, Canada.

Most recently, Chrispin Ntungo founded the Overseas African Magazine, which can be accessed at www.overseasafrican.com. By sharing immigrant experiences, the magazine's purpose is to inspire, motivate and empower Overseas Africans to be united, overcome challenges and achieve their dreams.

Chrispin Ntungo has a Ph.D. in Agricultural Economics from the University of Manitoba. He has been interviewed by the Canadian Broadcasting Corporation radio to highlight the accomplishments, challenges and dreams of Overseas Africans. He is also a well sought after speaker and contributor on issues affecting African communities on the Globe.

Printed in the United States
40210LVS00004B/331-360

9 781420 876246